TABLE OF CONTENTS

Page

ACRONYMS

ANA	Arab Northern Army
CIGS	Chief of the Imperial General Staff
CTC	Camel Transport Corps
DMC	Desert Mounted Corps
EEF	Egyptian Expeditionary Force
ELC	Egyptian Labor Corps
GOC	General Officer Commanding
LOCs	Lines of Communications
RAF	Royal Air Force
RFC	Royal Flying Corps
RNAS	Royal Naval Air Service

ILLUSTRATIONS

TABLE

CHAPTER 1

INTRODUCTION

<u>Allenby Enters Jerusalem, 1917</u>

By the end of 1917, the Allies were facing a dark period. The Italian offensive was reversed at Caporetto; the communist revolution caused the Russians to abandon the war; Romania withdrew; and the Germans launched a successful counteroffensive at Cambrai.[1] Yet in a separate corner of the world, there was another front of the Great War that was raging. The area was Palestine and a triumphant leader was driving the allies from victory to victory against the Turko-German forces defending there. His name was Sir Edmund Allenby and his force was the Egyptian Expeditionary Force (EEF).

In stark contrast to the gloom enshrouding the allies in Europe, Sir Edmund Allenby walked through the Jaffa gate into the historic city of Jerusalem on 11 December 1917. The capture of Jerusalem was a definitive point for the Palestinian front as it represented an important operational victory for Allenby and placed his forces at the doorstep of the Turko-German Force Headquarters. The victory also had a heartening effect on the morale of the Allies.

Egypt and Palestine offered the British an opportunity to fight a war of movement. Unlike the Western Front, Egypt and Palestine were undeveloped with wide expanses of land and low density of people and material. It was ripe for maneuver warfare using the mechanical products of the industrial age: motor cars, machine guns, tanks and aeroplanes. In particular, it was the use of aeroplanes that proved vital to the successful British defense of the Suez Canal by providing reconnaissance of enemy formations and early warnings of attack. This role of the Royal Flying Corps expanded in

1

this theater to cover the breadth and depth of British efforts at the tactical, operational and strategic levels of war.

Thesis: The actions of the Royal Air Force at the Battle of Megiddo were the culmination of three phases of development. Driven by capable leadership, and fueled by an ever-evolving aircraft manufacturing industry, the RAF quickly evolved as a learning organization able to capitalize on the emerging third dimension of warfare. What the RAF achieved at Megiddo was a systematic dominance of battlespace which contributed directly to the victory of Allied Forces in the Palestinian theater.

Significance of Megiddo
Translation of the Name

The name "Armageddon" connotes biblical references to the end of the world-- but it is also a location on the globe. The name Harmageddon or Armageddon derives from the Hebrew "Har," meaning tell or hill, and "Mageddon," referring to the ancient city of Megiddo. Therefore the name quite literally refers to the ruins of the ancient city of Megiddo--a city with a history of military significance. This significance was not lost on the forces arrayed in Palestine in September 1918. In fact, General Allenby's decisive Palestine campaign so closely resembled the strategy used by the Pharaoh Thutmose in 1457 B.C. that many historians debate whether Allenby was in fact replicating the ancient strategy. According to author and archaeologist Eric H. Cline, Allenby was aware of the history if Megiddo and of the campaign waged by the Pharaoh Thutmose III. Furthermore, according to Cline, Allenby was offered the honor to add "of Armageddon" to his title, but refused believing it to be too sensational. Instead, he accepted the more

2

benign title: "Allenby of Megiddo," thereby demonstrating his understanding of Megiddo's significance.

Geography of Megiddo

Megiddo sat upon key terrain in the ancient world. It is located at the mouth of the Musmuss Pass, half-way between the great cities of Nablus and Haifa, and twelve miles Southwest of Nazareth. It sits at the entrance to the vast Plain of Esdraelon (the Greek translation of Jezreel) and has a vantage of the pass and the plain all the way to Haifa some fifteen miles to the Northwest.[2] Most significant, though, is that Megiddo sat astride a great road intersection, connecting the coastal road from Egypt to Damascus and Mesopotamia. This road, known as the Via Maris (way of the sea), was one of the most important communication and trade routes of the ancient world[3] (see figure 1).

There were many famous and infamous historic figures associated with Megiddo: Solomon, Pharaoh Necho II, Saladin, and the Mamluke Sultan Qutuz (see appendix A). Yet of the many battles that were recorded to have been fought in the vicinity of Megiddo, there was one that bears the most significance to the actions of Allenby and the Egyptian Expeditionary Force of the First World War--Pharaoh Thutmose III. It was the details of this battle which bore the controversy over Allenby's decisions during his Palestine Campaign. Was he conscious of Thutmose III's victory at Megiddo and did he try to recreate it?

Pharaoh Thutmose III

Argued to be the first fully recorded battle in history, The Pharaoh Thutmose III fought the Canaanites at Megiddo in 1457 B.C. Pharaoh Thutmose III, the Sixth Pharaoh of Eighteenth Dynasty reigned from 1479 to 1425 B.C. He is regarded as one of the greatest Warrior Pharaohs, sometimes referred to as "Napoleon of Egypt."[4] His empire stretched from southern Syria, Canaan and through Nubia. Shortly after being declared Pharaoh, in 1457 B.C., he embarked on his first campaign against the King of Kadesh at Megiddo. He was 22 years old, and this was his first taste of battle.

Despite his councils trying to convince him otherwise, Thutmose used a narrow mountain pass, known as the Musmuss pass, to maneuver his army through and emerge between the Canaanite forces and the city of Megiddo. It was this decision that revealed Thutmose's tactical prowess. His choice was to either take the larger passes towards Megiddo to the North and South or to maneuver through a very narrow pass which would make his army vulnerable to a Canaanite ambush. Thutmose gambled that the Canaanites would also think like his council and expect him to come from the alternate Northern or Southern passes. His gamble paid off.

Battle occurred on 9 May, 1457 B.C. (based on his accession), the Canaanites escaped into Megiddo and Thutmose laid siege to the city for eight months. The battle that ensued was a complete and decisive victory for Thutmose, and is considered to be the largest of his seventeen campaigns. The successful campaign changed the political dynamics of the region. Thutmose III gained control of all of northern Canaan by taking Megiddo, and established an Egyptian presence in the Levant that lasted for the next two hundred years.[5]

Allenby

Until 1918, there was relatively little fighting on the hill of Megiddo. There was nothing of significance at Megiddo in September 1918 that the Allies were seeking to capture. There are no roads or rails that pass through it, nor are there any navigable rivers. The "significant" terrain were the towns of Tul Karm, Sebustiye and Nablus, which were major rail junctions Northwest of Jaffa; as well as the port of Haifa, and Samakh. The latter of which represented the juncture of the Palestinian Rail network and the Jordan River, where it meets Lake Tiberius. The significance of calling this battle Megiddo, which was to be the critical battle of the entire Palestinian Campaign and, indeed, the Middle-Eastern Theater, was the fact Megiddo became the epicenter of the British and Allied advance from Gaza to Aleppo. The latter being the location where the campaign ended when the Turks sued for peace and armistice.

Yet General Allenby's campaign does resemble the strategy employed by Thutmose III three millenniums ago. Allenby, like Thutmose, advanced with a force from Egypt and maneuvered his forces up the coast to attack the enemy forces arrayed in the

Jezreel valley. Allenby used all the resources at his disposal to overwhelm the Turkish defenders around Megiddo to include a new instrument of war –the airplane.

Importance of Airpower

The instrument of war that played such a prominent part in Allenby's Palestine Campaign had a very humble beginning. It is important to understand how rudimentary the aeroplane was at the outset of the war in order to gain an appreciation for how quickly it developed and how far it progressed.

The evolution of manned flight began as near fantasy at the turn of the century. But at the outset of war in 1914 it quickly developed to satiate military necessity. Prior to 1907, heavier-than-air flight was relegated to a club of fanciful dreamers who bankrolled their own projects and often wound up penniless. The Wright brothers' first flight at Kitty Hawk, North Carolina in December 1903, was a milestone for heavier-than-air flight, but was not the revolutionary catalyst for aviation enthusiasm. In fact, the Wright brothers spent a great deal of time and energy trying to convince the U.S. Congress to purchase a "flyer," but were rejected in January 1905. The Wrights then turned to European nations from 1905 to 1908 for aviation contracts. By December 1908, Wilbur Wright astounded spectators in France with his feats of aerobatics and flight duration--setting a record of 2 hours and 20 minutes of continuous flight. This record, coupled with the accomplishment of the French aviator Henri Farman, who flew his airplane almost 30 kilometers, from Bouy to Reims on 30 October 1908, had a dramatic effect on the development of aircraft. Now for the first time in the history of its development, heavier-than-air machines were demonstrating their military applicability, specifically, their suitability as a platform from which to conduct reconnaissance.[6]

During this same period of time, lighter-than-air aircraft were evolving on the world stage. While hot air balloons had first made their appearance in 1783, they where most successfully used throughout the nineteenth century as tethered observation platforms. Free flight of balloons, however, was a very difficult and unreliable method of flight. The emergence of the powered dirigible in 1884 changed this. By the turn of the twentieth century, Count Ferdinand von Zeppelin had developed a monstrous airship for the German General Staff. By 1907, Zeppelin had designed an airship over 128 meters long, with a volume of 11,300 cubic meters capable of flying over 350 kilometers in under eight hours.[7] This captured the attention of the world--especially Britain.

Always concerned about an invasion from the European mainland, Britain grew ever-more concerned about the aviation developments east of the Rhine. This concern was fueled by H.G. Wells, who published his *War in the Air* in 1907; and by Sir Charles Rolls, of the Rolls Royce Company, who testified before the Committee of Imperial Defense that due to aviation developments "England will cease to be an Island."[8] It was under these circumstances that the aeroplane emerged on the European stage in 1908. It was evolving from romantic endeavor to military necessity.

By 1909 aviation was an emerging industry. Companies sprang up all over the world to design, build, test, and sell their aircraft to governments concerned about keeping pace with their potential adversaries. During this same year, the importance and usefulness of dirigibles began to wane. The German General Staff itself was beginning to note the military inadequacies of the Zeppelin airships. Yet, the Zeppelin was a symbol of German pride, ingenuity and engineering and Germany was not ready to scrap the airship. Instead, Germany divided its efforts between the continued development of airships as well as aeroplanes.

Germany's distraction and pride in the development and production of Zeppelins caused her to ignore, for the most part, the advances in aeroplanes and aeroplane technology that were taking place elsewhere in Europe. Ironically, the threat that the Zeppelins posed to France and Britain was the catalyst for those countries to develop aeroplanes as a counter-threat. As a result, Britain had aircraft in Egypt in defense of the Suez Canal in 1914. These aircraft were unopposed.

While the aircraft industry tested and experimented with various aeroplane designs, the airmen and military commanders experimented with developing roles for this new weapon of war. The Royal Flying Corps, like other air forces in its day, developed three roles for their aircraft: reconnaissance, air-ground integration, and denying enemy air capabilities.

Reconnaissance

> [The airplane's] first duty was reconnaissance. All its other and later uses were consequences of this central purpose, and were forced on it by the hard logic of events.[9]

> Sir Walter Raleigh, *The War in the Air*

In the First World War the airmen proved their usefulness, if not their indispensability. The airmen gave eyes to the army. In their efforts against the Russians, German observation planes played a vital role in the victory at Tannenberg, to which Field Marshal von Hindenburg commented, "Without the airmen no Tannenberg."[10] The airmen serving in the Palestine Brigade of the Royal Flying Corps were absolutely

9

critical to the success in that theater. Mastery of the skies meant, most of all, knowledge of the enemy's positions and possible intentions through aerial reconnaissance.

As previously mentioned, the usefulness of aerial reconnaissance dates back to the hot air balloon. The foremost mission of the aeroplane was reconnaissance. Direct incorporation of aircraft with ground forces began in 1910, when the British Army used civilian aviators to participate in maneuvers on Salisbury Plain. This was the first time that reconnaissance was carried out by airplane. After this many other countries performed similar experiments. In 1911, the French, who were far ahead of the British in aircraft manufacturing and aeronautical science, carried out maneuvers in Picardy and confirmed the value of the airplane for reconnaissance purposes. Furthermore, the French noted that single-seat airplanes had to fly twice as much for its pilots to bring back the same amount of information supplied by the two-seated variants--carrying a pilot and an observer.[11] Squadrons of these two-seated observation planes were introduced in 1912, and quickly became the preferred aerial reconnaissance configuration.

The development of the reconnaissance mission for the airmen meant the development of techniques to capture the information that was observed and then to be able to communicate this information to the user in a timely manner. In the early days of the war, the pilots would rapidly sketch what they observed and then drop this information to the awaiting courier on the ground as they flew over. But this method was quickly replaced by the photograph. By 1914, aerial photography had already been used for approximately fifty years. So the technique proved to be extremely valuable in providing detailed information of enemy positions and possible intentions. Some of these cameras were capable of taking a series of photographs. Dubbed automatic cameras,

10

these cameras provided a storybook gallery of the area being observed.[12] One of the pioneers of this technology was Gioulio Douhet, who would distinguish himself after the war with his book entitled *The Command of the Air*.

Many countries carried out military maneuvers incorporating aircraft from 1910 to 1914, and virtually all identified the limiting factor of the airplane in reconnaissance--communication. The U.S. Army used airplanes in small-scale maneuvers in 1912 and determined that the information was much more accurate and full than that obtained by the cavalry. However, it also noted that the observers had no rapid or easy means to relay their information to the ground.[13] The only logical solution was to incorporate wireless telegraph into the cockpits. But this technology needed to be refined for use in aircraft.

The Germans followed suit with two-seated observations planes. This division of duties in the cockpit allowed for more reliable information and better photographs. In fact, the photographic information supplied by aerial observers became so ubiquitous that by 1916 photographic intelligence was being passed down to brigade headquarters. By the end of the war, photographs of objectives were even passed down to the trenches![14] After the war, the Germans calculated that if all the aerial photographs they had made were laid out, they would cover an area six times larger than Germany.[15]

Air-Ground Integration

While photographs proved to be an important part of intelligence gathering, the observation aircraft also provided a critical role in rapidly developing situations. After 1916, observation aircraft would often be called upon to work in cooperation with the infantry, in order to provide information to the headquarters of the infantry's progress on the battlefield during offenses.[16] As Allenby's forces attacked up the Plain of Sharon in

11

1918, observation aircraft flew out in front of each corps and reported any enemy observations to the corps' lead elements.[17] The observation aircraft also proved to be a valuable tool for evaluating the effects of artillery and communicating corrections to the gunners. Eventually, the airplane was used to perform the task for which it was most feared--bombing and ground-attack. Therefore, the role of air-ground integration was comprised of three sub-tasks: artillery spotting, bombing, and ground attack.

Artillery spotting

Tethered balloons had been in service in most armies throughout the second half of the nineteenth century. These balloons performed a valuable function for artillery. Since the range of artillery was increasing to the point that the artillerists were no longer able to view the effectiveness of their fires, observers in balloons performed this function. This was a dangerous business since the balloons were obvious targets for enemy guns as well as aircraft. The French artillery had pushed to acquire aircraft for their purposes as early as 1909. The Italians had assigned a unit out of the Italian air service to develop spotting techniques in 1912.[18]

Prior to the outset of the war, most countries that possessed airplanes were experimenting with spotting techniques. Reliable and timely communication between the observers and artillerymen remained as the limiting factor to the airplane's effectiveness in artillery spotting. Early in the war, most pilots dropped notes with sketches or map indications to the artillerymen. When the conditions permitted, some pilots would simply land their planes near the gun positions and discuss their observations with the artillerymen face-to-face.[19] These techniques were time-consuming. Like the dilemma involved with the aerial reconnaissance mission, what was needed was a means for the

12

pilots to communicate with the ground while they were observing the rounds impacting.

Again, the answer was wireless telegraphy.

At first these wireless systems were bulky and unreliable. But by late 1915, wireless transmitters had become fixtures on observation aircraft flying over the Western and Italian Fronts.[20] The greatest limitation of the wireless system was that the pilots could not receive information in the cockpit. But these difficulties were eventually worked out and the airplane proved to be more reliable in the artillery spotting role than balloons mostly because of its range, versatility of view, and the fact that it could fly on windy days.

Evidence of the evolution of the role of artillery spotting into normal operations is found in the communiqués of the British Royal Flying Corps. In 1915, most of the efforts of artillery spotting or cooperation are noted as separate entries, such as the following report listed under the title "Artillery co-operation" in Communiqué No. 2, 26-31 July 1915:

> 2Lt Reid with Lt Russell, 2 Sqn, obtained a direct hit in a gun emplacement when registering for the 10th Battery.
> Capt Collins and Lt Sweet registering for 3rd Bde, obtained two direct hits on and set fire a portion of the enemy's works
> On the 28th July, a machine of I Sqn directed battery fire on an ammunition column. A direct hit blew up the depot.[21]

By 1916 the reports involving artillery cooperation were simply part of the dated activity and not given separate consideration or notation. The effectiveness of the cooperation was also becoming more catastrophic as evidenced by the following communiqué dated 2 August 1916:

> Eighty-six targets were engaged with aeroplane observation and 8 with kite balloon with very successful results.

Twelve batteries were successfully dealt with by the Reserve Army artillery observed by machines of the XVth Wing, and 7 by the IVth Army and 4th Brigade.

Direct hits were seen on 9 gun emplacements, and explosions were caused in nine cases, one being very extensive.[22]

One of the most important adaptations for artillery spotting was the development of grid-square systems. This system which was in use by the French as early as 1911, divided maps into geometric squares which were identified by pairs of numbers. Similar to the grid reference system still in use today. W.G. H. Salmond, who would become the commander of the Royal Flying Corps in Palestine, worked out a system of artillery-to-air cooperation based on this squared map, which was adopted by the Royal Flying Corps in France. The system was dubbed "Major Salmond's System."[23] As the officer responsible for the development, training and success of the RFC's Palestine Brigade, Salmond frequently gave classes on the subject as well as general cooperation between the RFC and the other arms which fostered cooperation throughout the EEF[24]

Bombing

The fear of attack from the heavens predates the emergence of the airplane. Perhaps it was the desire to harness this capability that drove the development of powered flight. In any event, the capability to effectively bomb targets deep in the enemy's rear from the air was arguably the most predictable development of aerial warfare and the most feared. However, this capability was not immediately available at the outset of the First World War. By the end of the war, however, effective bombing of carefully planned ground targets were very effective and proved to be decisive in the Battle of Megiddo.

While the ominous airships captured the public attention during the first weeks of the war, it was the airplane that made routine bombing a reality.[25] The dirigibles proved

14

to be vulnerable to air as well as ground attack and therefore did not provide the strategic reconnaissance and bombing capabilities for which it was designed. Instead, the bombing capabilities evolved out of the airplane squadrons. As early as September 1914, the Royal Flying Corps issued orders for all reconnaissance pilots to carry bombs. The French also saw the value in allowing the observation aircraft to perform bombing missions, but the French recognized the importance of organizing units specifically for this duty. Late in 1914, the French combined three escadrilles (flying squadrons) to form Groupe De Bombardement No. 1 (G.B. 1).[26]

By 1915, bombers became an extension of artillery--being able to strike at targets 30 or more miles behind enemy lines and on the reverse slopes of hills.[27] But there was a strategic purpose for bombing that was beginning to manifest itself in the capabilities demonstrated by the early and rudimentary "bombers." In March 1915, the British used bombers at the battle of Neuve-Chapelle. They concentrated their efforts on the railway stations and junctions. Although the results were not dramatic, they did serve to slow the flow of men and munitions to the front lines. In spring of that same year, the Germans began using gas at Ypres, Belgium. In response, the French bombed the Badische Analin und Soda Fabrik, where they believed that the Germans were producing chlorine gas.[28]

The groundwork had thus been laid for the need to develop an airplane capable of longer range and greater bomb load capacity. These aircraft, such as the British Handley-Page 0/100 and German Gothas became available in 1916.

Ground Attack

As the war continued to evolve, a new role for aircraft emerged--ground-attack. Aircraft were serving in contact patrols in which they would follow closely with advancing ground forces providing reports to the headquarters on progress. From their unique vantage points the aircraft would often drop notes to the advancing units informing them of enemy strong-points or obstacles ahead. The aircraft performing these missions were often two-seat observation aircraft that had to fly low in order to distinguish friendly from enemy forces.[29] The logical effect was that these aircraft would at times engage threats or gun emplacements in support of the ground forces. Therefore, it seems that the ground-attack role emerged from individual initiative.[30] Nevertheless, it was not long before the method was adopted and incorporated into the war plans.

The first evidence of official sanction for the ground-attack role was during the Battle of the Somme in 1916. The Royal Flying Corps assigned eighteen contact planes with the task of providing close reconnaissance and bombardment.[31] Ground-attack became a more accepted use of air power late in the war, specifically in the campaigns of 1918 when large numbers of troops were out of their trenches and on the roads.[32] Simply stated, this form of attack used machine gun fire to strafe targets on the ground while reserving small bombs for vehicles and buildings.

The Germans were the first to develop units specifically for the ground-attack mission. These *Schlachtstaffeln* were two-seater aircraft which served as armed escorts.[33] These units were employed at the decisive point of the attack where the commander on the ground believed they would have the greatest effect. Furthermore, these aircraft would often fly in formation at minimum altitude in order the "shatter the enemy's nerve."[34] This role continued to evolve throughout the rest of the war, to include cooperation with tank units in attack--as the precursor to the modern concept of close air support.

16

Deny Enemy Air Capabilities

When considering the evolution of air capabilities and potential for destruction, an elementary question emerges: How could the Allies in World War I keep from being vulnerable to attack from the air? There were two ways: passive and active. Passive air defense implied camouflaging equipment, movement of equipment and personnel undercover or underground, hardening of sites to deflect enemy bombs, or otherwise prevent observation or affects by the enemy from the air. Active air defense implied destroying or chasing away enemy aircraft. This proved to be the more difficult proposition. In order to accomplish active air defense, the Allies needed to have the capability to destroy the enemy's aircraft. Furthermore, they needed know the locations of the enemy's aircraft.

In his book entitled, *Command of the Air*, Giulio Douhet wrote: "in order to conquer the command of the air, it is necessary to destroy all of the enemy's means of flying."[35] While Douhet had the benefit of hindsight, this first and foremost mission of an air force was not immediately realized in World War I. Instead the world witnessed the slow revelation of this necessity. In fact there are some in Britain who are surprised to still be in the fight by 1915. The editor of *The Aeroplane*, C. G. Grey wrote in 1915: "That Germany has failed to obtain command of the air is a curious freak of fate. By all rules our little air fleet ought to have ceased to exist, along with our 'contemptible little Army', about a week after the war was declared."[36]

This understanding of destroying the enemy's air capabilities was understood well before the war. In 1913, Winston Churchill, then Lord of the Admiralty, argued in the face of the Zeppelin craze that the best antidote to air attack was not through passive defense but through active bombing of the enemy's aerodromes on the ground. He believed that the Zeppelins were far more vulnerable to bombing attacks in their sheds than to anything that might be mustered against them while in the air.[37] Evidence of this was in the successful bombing raids carried out by the Royal Naval Air Service (RNAS) against the dirigible shed at Dusseldorf in September and October 1914. In which they succeeded in destroying both the shed and the dirigible inside.[38]

In the final analysis, it was imperative to deny the enemy air capability or to at least minimize its effectiveness in order to then exploit the command of the air. This was either accomplished through the destruction of the enemy's aircraft or the destruction of the enemy's aerodromes/airfields, or both. According to Giulio Douhet, "it is not enough to shoot down all the birds in flight if you want to wipe out the species; there remain the eggs and the nests."[39]

What the Royal Air Force accomplished in Palestine in 1918 was a brilliant combination of both passive and active air defense. While the superior numbers and matched quality of the British aircraft prevented the Germans from passing over the lines, the EEF also took great pains to camouflage and hide their equipment from aerial observation. The RAF flew missions over friendly lines and photographed positions to verify the passive defensive efforts and assist in the correction of shortcomings.[40]

Overall Effect

Air power evolved throughout World War I. By war's end, both sides produced better machines, developed better tactics and reaped better results when compared to the beginning of the war. While both sides understood the importance of achieving command of the air, it remained an illusive goal for much of the war. Any advantage in air power that one side achieved, through some innovation, was often short lived and not fully coordinated or exploited with other plans or tactics on the ground--with exception.

In the small "sideshow" of the war called Palestine, the Allies demonstrated the effective use of all elements of combat power working in synchronized concert to have an overwhelming and decisive impact on the war. The Palestine campaign is a microcosm of World War I, in which both sides were locked in a stalemate while struggling to implement all the technologies emerging from the industrial age. What the campaign in Palestine shows us is that when all the air resources are pulled together under one command and that force focuses on first denying the enemy's air capability through systematic destruction, then that air force had achieved battlespace dominance and freedom of action to conduct effective reconnaissance and ground interdiction of the enemy. Furthermore, once the command of the air was achieved, the ground commander had the freedom to maneuver his forces without detection and thus achieve surprise. Such was the legacy of the battle of Megiddo in 1918.

<u>The Road To War In Palestine</u>

Almost as soon as the guns of August sounded in 1914, the British War Ministry was concerned with the possible entry of Turkey into the war. Britain began posturing and preparing for such an occasion, while also trying to not antagonize Turkish involvement. Moreover, Britain needed the support of Arabs that were spread throughout the Middle East and North Africa if they were going to have to defend their interests and possessions in those areas. On 26 September 1914, General Sir E. Barrow, Military Secretary of the India Office, wrote an appreciation of the developing situation, entitled "The Role of India in a Turkish War,"

19

> All the omens point to war with Turkey within a few weeks or even days. Such a contingency need not alarm us unless the Turks succeed in drawing the Arabs to their side. In that case they will proclaim a *Jahad* and endeavor to raise Afghanistan and the frontier tribes against us, which might be a serious danger to India and would most certainly add enormously to our difficulties and responsibilities. This shows how important it is to us to avoid a Turco-Arab coalition.[41]

With this understanding, General Barrow began to mobilize and organize an Indian force to answer the British Empire's call. It was important for Britain to show a military presence in the strategic locations such as the Shatt Al Arab and the Suez in order to encourage the Arab support of British interests. Without the Arab support, Turkey's hope for a Jihad against the British would be impossible.[42]

Turkey was divided on the subject of entering the war. The Germans were entrenched in the debate, as German and Austrian Ambassadors continued to increase their efforts to involve Turkey. According to the British Ambassador to Turkey, Sir L. Mallet, "the Turks did not intend to make war with Britain, but they were falling in line with German designs in order to extract as much as possible from Germany. . .and that Enver Pasha had ambitious schemes in the Arab world and in Egypt."[43]

Egypt was critical to the British Empire, because of the Suez Canal. This canal linked Britain to her possessions in India, Australia and Asia. It was the narrow jugular for her lines of communication, supplies and personnel. The successful capture and control of this canal could, therefore, cripple the British war effort on the Western Front. It was imperative that Britain retain uninterrupted shipping through the Suez. As the war party in Turkey gained the upper hand, Britain continued to prepare itself for what seemed to be the inevitable involvement of Turkey in the war.

Turkey's fate was determined on 29 October, 1914 as the German naval ships *Goeben* and *Breslau* along with some Turkish destroyers, entered the Black sea and bombarded several Russian ports. Russia declared war on Turkey on 2 November, France and Britain made their declarations on 5 November.[44] Once their alliance with the Ottoman Empire was secured in November of 1914, the Germans prodded the Turks to attack the Suez Canal. Thus the competition for the Middle-East ensued, as the forces on each side gradually developed and mobilized their relative strengths in the region.

This struggle in the Middle East, specifically in Egypt and Palestine resulted in three distinct phases that were characterized and distinguished by leadership, tactics, training, and operations.

---

[1]Cyril Falls, *Military Operations Egypt and Palestine from June 1917 to the End of the War,* Vol. 1 (London: H. M. Stationary Office, 1930), 265.

[2]E. H. Cline, *The Battles of Armageddon: Megiddo and the Jezreel Valley from the Bronze Age to the Nuclear Age* (Ann Arbor: University of Michigan Press., 2000), 7.

[3]Israeli Foreign Ministry. "Megiddo - The Solomonic Chariot City." *Jewish Virtual Library* (Available from: http://www.jewishvirtuallibrary.org/jsource/ Archaeology/Megiddo.html, accessed online 24 March 2007).

[4]J. H. Breasted, *Ancient Times: A History of the Early World; an Introduction to the Study of Ancient History and the Career of Early Man*, Outlines of European History 1. (Boston: Ginn and Company, 1914), 85.

[5]Cline, 22.

[6]John H. Morrow, *The Great War in the Air* (Washington: Smithsonian Institute Press, 1993), 8.

[7]Ibid., 3.

[8]Ibid., 4.

[9]Sir Walter Raleigh, *The War in the Air: Being the Story of the Part Played in the Great War by the Royal Air Force,* Vol. 1 (Oxford: Clarendon Press, 1922), 213.

[10]Lee B. Kennett, *The First Air War, 1914-1918* (New York: The Free Press, 1991), 32.

[11]Ibid., 17.

[12]Ibid., 37.

[13]Ibid., 17.

[14]Ibid., 37.

[15]Ibid., 38.

[16]Ibid.

[17]Falls, 523.

[18]Kennett, 33.

[19]Ibid., 33.

[20]Ibid., 34.

[21]Chistopher Cole, ed., *Royal Flying Corps Communiqués, 1915-1916* (London: Tom Donovan Publishing, Ltd., 1969), 21.

[22]Ibid., 205.

[23]Anne Baker, *From Biplanes to Spitfires: The Life of Air Chief Marshal Sir Geoffrey Salmond* (S. Yorkshire: Pen & Sword Books, 2003), 49.

[24]Ibid., 85.

[25]Kennett, 47.

[26]Ibid., 49.

[27]Ibid., 48.

[28]Ibid., 49.

[29]Ibid., 211.

[30]Ibid.

[31]Ibid.

[32]Ibid., 212.

[33] Ibid., 211.

[34] Ibid.

[35] Giulio Douhet, *The Command of the Air,* trans. Dino Ferrari (New York: Coward-McCann, 1942; reprint, 1983), 34.

[36] Harald Penrose, *British Aviation: The Great War and Armistice, 1915-1919* (London: Putnam, 1969), 12.

[37] Malcom Cooper, *The Birth of Independent Air Power: British Air Policy in the First World War* (London: Allen & Unwin, Inc., 1986), 50.

[38] Kennett, 50.

[39] Douhet, 34.

[40] Falls, 462.

[41] F. J. Moberly, *The Campaign in Mesopotamia, 1914-1918*, Vol. 1 (London: HMSO, 1923), 86.

[42] Ibid., 87.

[43] Ibid., 96.

[44] Ibid., 98.

CHAPTER 2

PHASE I: AUGUST 1914 TO FEBRUARY 1916

This first phase of operations in Egypt and Palestine was, essentially, a defensive economy-of-force effort on the part of the British. Although the Suez Canal in Egypt was vitally important to the British, they could not afford to send their best leaders and equipment away from the "big" fight in Europe. However, their decisions did make sense. The British did place in command an officer who had a great deal of experience in the region, and they did send a sufficient size force to defend the canal. The British also sent aircraft to Egypt in order to provide early warning of an attack on the canal. It was this small compliment of aircraft that gave the British the important edge they needed to thwart the Turkish plans and efforts to seize the canal. By the end of this phase the British learned a valuable lesson regarding the use of aeroplanes in defensive operations--aerial reconnaissance was essential to an effective defense against a superior force.

Leadership

Commander-in-Chief Egypt, Lieutenant-General Sir John Maxwell

John Grenfell Maxwell received his commission on 22 March 1879 in the 42nd Highlanders Regiment. He distinguished himself throughout his career and spent a good amount of time in Egypt. He commanded the 2nd Egyptian Brigade in 1898, and the 14th Brigade in South Africa. He was knighted in 1900 and appointed as Military Governor of Pretoria (1900-01). Then he returned to Egypt in 1908 as the General Officer Commanding (GOC) British Troops, and remained in that post until 1912. In the prosecution of his duties, Maxwell also gained a reputation as an Egyptologist.[1]

When the "guns of August" sounded in 1914, Maxwell was 55 years old and not in command. He expected a choice assignment, since his friend, Lord Herbert Kitchener, was now Secretary of State for War; but it did not come. He traveled to France in the beginning of the War as head of the British Military Mission to the French Army GHQ. He remained on the Western Front until just after the First Battle of the Marne. In September 1914, he returned to Egypt as Commander-in-Chief. Yet Maxwell never really seemed satisfied at his position. He regarded it as "little better than Quartermaster General of the Army . . . providing endless training and supplies to troops destined for Gallipoli, Salonika and Palestine."[2]

By 1915 Egypt was indeed growing into a key staging and logistics base for operations in the peripheries. But Maxwell continued to feel as though he was not being permitted to influence strategy. By spring of 1916, he requested to be relieved of command and return home. His transfer took place in March 1916. His subsequent assignment was as the Commander-In-Chief of Ireland--just in time for the Easter Rebellion of 1916. He was notorious for his harsh treatment of Irish prisoners to include the executions of rebel leaders and the imposition of martial law. He was promoted to General in 1919, and retired from service in 1922. General John G. Maxwell died in 1929.

As the first commander of the British forces in Egypt, Maxwell was a good choice due to his experience in the region. However, by 1914 Maxwell had spent almost too much time there. Instead of facing his command in Egypt with enthusiasm and optimism, Maxwell viewed it more like a sentence that he was serving. He had not spent time on the Western Front, and although he had coordinated a very successful defense of the canal he skulked as if he was being left out of the war. The commanders that followed Maxwell took a more energetic and optimistic approach to the command, which represented a fresh opportunity in a stagnant war.

Initial Flight Commander, Captain S. D. Massey

As the British began to make preparations in defense of the Suez, a flight of aeroplanes was dispatched from Britain on 4 November 1914--the day before Britain formally declared war on Turkey.[3] The intent of these aeroplanes was to conduct essential aerial reconnaissance of Turkish positions to provide early warning to the British forces defending the canal. This small force was commanded by Captain S.D. Massey.

Massey had been in command of the Indian Flying School at Sitapur since 1913. He arrived at Alexandria, Egypt on 17 November with three Maurice Farman pusher aeroplanes. In addition to these, two old but air-worthy Henri Farmans were acquired from an Italian firm in Cairo. Massey was given a site for his aerodrome at Ismailia, which was an ideal location in the center of the Canal Zone (see figure 2). Contractors from Cairo soon began erecting sheds to house the aircraft. Massey wasted little time. He launched his first reconnaissance flight on 27 November and maintained frequent surveillance of the canal zone area and out East to a range of about 45 miles.[4]

In December the first mechanics and an engineer for the Ismailia flight arrived from the Indian Flying School at Sitpur. They brought with them one B.E.2a and two Maurice Faraman aeroplanes--all without engines. At about the same time, three pilots arrived from Britain bringing with them two Renault engines and miscellaneous supplies.[5]

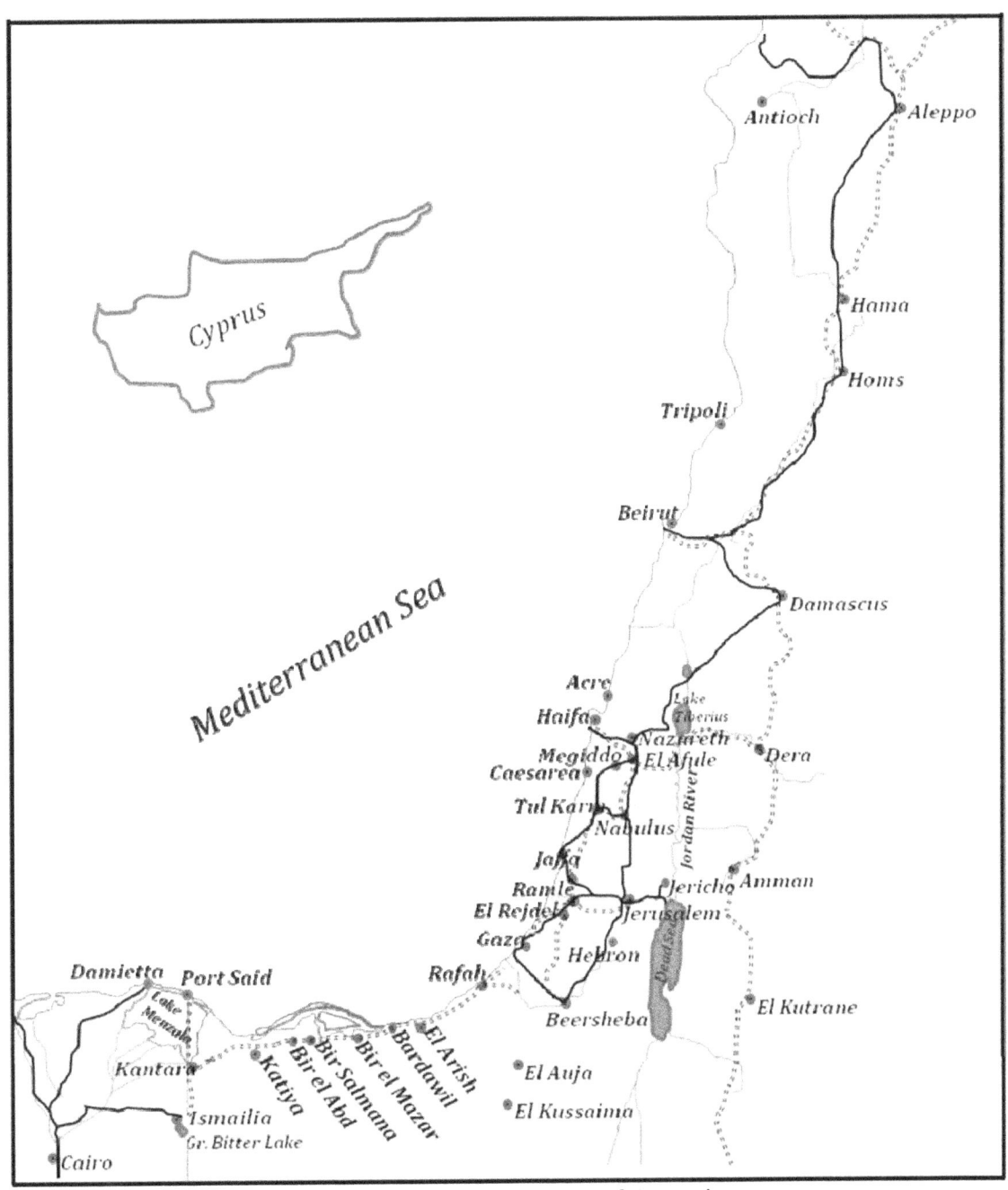

Figure 1.   Map of EEF Area of Operations

What Captain Massey did for the RFC in Egypt was to provide a good

springboard for the many operations to follow. Getting the airmen involved immediately into the effort of the canal's defense was not only critical to the operation but was also critical to the establishment of the organization. It gave the airmen a sense of purpose as well as the reputation for willingness to work hard and conduct operations in even the harshest conditions. The commanders that followed Massey continued to build upon this reputation until the RFC in Egypt was an integral and critical part of the British Forces there.

Lieutenant-Colonel W. G. H. Salmond

William Geoffrey Salmond graduated from Woolwich and was commissioned in the Royal Artillery at the age of 19. He was the son of Major General Sir William Salmond--a heroic officer who was knighted in 1902 for his part in the South African war. Geoffrey, as he was known to family and friends, spent his first assignment in South Africa where he was first exposed to the use of observation balloons that worked in conjunction with artillery. Geoffrey Salmond spent another year in South Africa and a year in China during the Boxer rebellion. He was accepted to the Staff College in 1910 where he became obsessed with flying and began to read anything he could get his hands on regarding the subject. He graduated from staff college in 1912 and attached to the 8th Hussars in Amesbury.[6]

It was during his time at Amesbury that Geoffrey Salmond first took to the skies. He volunteered himself on several occasions to serve as an observer on test flights from Larkhill field. Then began flying lessons with the Sopwith Flying School at Brooklands in 1912. The school was started by Thomas Octavius Sopwith, who would go on to develop the Sopwith Airplane Company and contribute greatly to the British aeronautical industry. Salmond completed his basic flight training in 1913 at the Central Flying

28

School at Upavon and was awarded his Royal Flying Corps Flight Certificate on 6 March 1913.[7] On 12 April, Captain Salmond received orders to report to the War Office to work on the Staff of General Sir David Henderson, who was the newly appointed Director of Military Aeronautics.[8] Geoffrey Salmond's career in the RFC was off to a promising start.

On 9 August 1914, Geoffrey Salmond departed for France to establish the RFC headquarters there. Upon his arrival, the British army was facing the onslaught of the German offensive and was in retreat from Maubeuge on 16 August 1914. The retreat continued from Maubeuge to Melun from 16 August to 4 September, with the RFC headquarters moving nine times in ten days. He was promoted to Major on 12 November 1914. In January 1915, he was given command of No. 1 Squadron, whose origins date to the very start of British Aviation.

Shortly after taking command of the Squadron, the Battle of Neuve Chapelle was launched. Salmond's Squadron was given the task of strategic reconnaissance and bombing of special military objectives.[9] The battle of Neuve Chapelle was the first time that aeroplanes were used in a specific bombing role. Shortly after this battle, Geoffrey Salmond was working closely with the artillery to identify and neutralize the German guns. It was during this time that Salmond noticed the problems and difficulties between air and artillery.[10] Being both an artillery officer and a pilot placed Salmond in the unique position to understand both sides of the equation. He developed a plan for integrating air and artillery which he produced in pamphlet form and briefed to the highest levels. The plan was first incorporated in the battle of Loos in April 1915 and then was adopted all along the front.[11]

On 18 August 1915, Geoffrey Salmond was promoted to Temporary Lieutenant Colonel and given the command of Fifth Wing. This wing was stationed at Gosport and was preparing for departure to Egypt. The wing consisted of two squadrons, Numbers 14 and 17, which were equipped with B.E. 2c aeroplanes and support equipment. In November 1915, Lieutenant Colonel Salmond and his "handful of aeroplanes" arrived in Port Said and immediately began to assemble and prepare the aeroplanes for operations. Salmond set up his headquarters in Heliopolis, which was located between Cairo and Ismailia. He sent "A" flight from 14 Squadron to replace 30 Squadron which departed for Mesopotamia in October.[12] Fifth Wing was the only air support available to all forces in the Middle East. Salmond assumed the duty of cooperation of air assets with ground forces and conducted operations in a manner that was described as "close, cordial and informed."[13]

Equipment

British

The aircraft that the British initially sent in defense of the Suez Canal were some of the oldest types that they possessed--Maurice and Henry Farman aeroplanes. These machines were little better than box-kite aircraft, but had an endurance of over three hours of continuous flight. This made a great difference in reconnaissance efforts. Furthermore, the fact that the British had aircraft when the Turks did not, made the age and obsolescence of these aircraft irrelevant.

The British also had support of a few Nieuport 4G aircraft which were in service with the Royal Navy. These aircraft were equipped with float landing gear and provided vital reconnaissance for Maxwell along the northern edges of the Sinai. Reconnaissance missions by these aircraft began in December 1914, and continued through to March 1915. However, as the Gallipoli campaign began in February 1915, many of these aircraft and their associated vessels departed the shores of the Sinai. There was a sharp decline in the availability of reconnaissance aircraft during this time.

Finally, the British had the very capable B.E. 2 (Bleroit Experimental version 2). The B.E. 2c was introduced in 1914 and featured built up cockpits, modified wing and tail configurations (designed to provide a more stable reconnaissance platform), and a Lewis machine gun for the observer. This aircraft would become the workhorse for the Royal Air Corps in the EEF until the spring of 1916 when the German planes began to arrive in theater. These British aeroplanes quickly proved to be no match for the German planes. The edge that the British had enjoyed over their enemy for over a year was lost.

German

The Germans were relatively late to incorporate aircraft into the Palestinian theater of operations. In fact, no aircraft were used in support of the Turkish attacks against the Suez Canal in 1915. The first German aircraft began to arrive in Palestine in the Spring of 1916. The allies first noticed the presence of German planes when seaplanes from the aircraft carrier Ben-my-Chree made a reconnaissance mission on 7 March 1916, over Beersheba and photographed an aerodrome with six hangars that had been erected near the town. This was in fact, the 300th Squadron, a German air unit from Hamburg, Germany. They were equipped with fourteen Rumpler aircraft.[14]

By this time in the war both sides began to realize that the war on the peripheries could have an important impact on the war in Europe. So this introduction of German aircraft into the Palestinian theater is indicative of the shift in German Strategy. The types of aircraft that the Germans provided were the very latest. And this fact would be used by the British proponents to argue for comparable equipment to be sent to Egypt.

Training and Tactics

The Royal Flying Corps was established by Royal Warrant on 13 May 1912, and the Central Flying School at Upavon began teaching military flying in August. Many of the pilots that were accepted into those first few classes already had some civilian flight training that they privately funded. Much of the early training took place in Farman style aeroplanes and many of the first flyers came from the Royal Engineers.[15]

For the balance of 1914, most of the missions assigned to the RFC were for reconnaissance of enemy positions. In Egypt, the first reconnaissance flight took place on 27 November 1914, and these flights provided extremely valuable operational information. While there was some bombing of Turkish forces in that initial phase of the war, these tactics were mostly used as harassment measures and did not have a decisive impact. The bombing tactics were initially the rudimentary practice of tossing grenades from the cockpit while flying over the target. This evolved by early 1915 to the practice of strapping 20 pound bombs to the underside of the wings or fuselage of the reconnaissance aircraft. But even the enemy admitted that these bombing attacks "at first caused panic among the men. . .but they soon got used to it."[16]

In 1915, several developments were emerging in the manner in which aeroplanes were employed in combat. While on the European continent there were improvements in artillery and air cooperation, thanks to the plan introduced by Major Salmond; in Egypt the RFC was improving and refining its reconnaissance and ground-attack methods. The operations in the Western Desert and in Darfur were providing the RFC valuable training opportunities rich with targets while the action along the canal zone grew stagnant. The British pilots were developing techniques of sketching enemy positions and relaying this information to ground forces. In one instance, RFC pilots coordinated their reconnaissance operations with the British sloop *Clematis* which fired on Senussi targets 10,000 yards away, causing the enemy to rout.[17]

As the allies evacuated the Gallipoli peninsula in January 1916, Egypt began to take on renewed importance and interest. In February, Lieutenant Colonel Salmond moved the Fifth Wing headquarters to Ismailia, where the new commander of British Forces in Egypt, Lieutenant General Murray, had set up his headquarters. Soon after setting up at Ismailia, Lieutenant Colonel Salmond began "a course of lectures for military officers, two days a week, to explain the organization of the Royal Flying Corps and its methods of cooperation with other arms."[18] These lectures grew in popularity and helped to foster a spirit of cooperation and sympathy between the arms.

From their introduction into Egypt in November 1914 until April 1916, the RFC was able to conduct operations fairly unmolested. By mid-April 1916, the first German aeroplanes were seen over the Sinai and these aircraft, mostly Rumplers and Fokkers, began to interdict the British aerial reconnaissance aircraft. Lieutenant Colonel Salmond remarked in a letter to his wife: "German aeroplanes have appeared and are making things much more lively."[19]

Organization and Operations

The organization of the RFC in Egypt evolved as the force grew in both quality and quantity of machines and pilots during this first phase of the war in the Palestinian Theater. Once the first aircraft and crews disembarked in Alexandria, Egypt on 17

November 1914 they were moved to Ismailia (see figure 4). This was a good location for

the reconnaissance aircraft. It was in the center of the Suez Canal zone right at the

western bank of the canal (see figure 5). It gave the reconnaissance pilots the ability to

range the entire canal zone.

This initial aerial reconnaissance unit was referred to as the Ismailia flight, under

the command of Captain Massey. This group became known as 30th Squadron from 24

March 1915.[20] In conjunction with the French Nieuport seaplanes operating from off the coast of the Sinai, this was the strategic reconnaissance available to Maxwell prior to the first attack on the canal in 1915.[21]

In December 1914 through January 1915, seaplane reconnaissance reported increasing concentrations of Turkish troops in the vicinity of Beersheba. This information coupled with information from spies, allowed the British command to conclude that the attack against the canal was imminent.[22] By the middle of January, most of the reconnaissance missions from Ismailia were uneventful. On 17 January 1915, a reconnaissance flight discovered the Turkish northern flanking column at Bir el Abd. Subsequent missions revealed the Turkish forces departing Beersheba and moving towards the canal--with the main effort against Ismailia. The reconnaissance missions continued and the reports of Turkish movements continue to flow into British headquarters. Then on 3 February the Turks' first attempt to cross the canal began as groups of men with pontoons and rafts advanced toward the canal south of Lake Timsah.[23] They were met with rifle and machine gun fire until most of them abandoned the effort and left their pontoons and rafts at the shoreline. A total of three pontoons crossed the canal, but their occupants were quickly killed or taken prisoner.[24]

The Turks did not conduct an immediate counter-attack against the canal. Instead, aeroplane reports on 4 February revealed that the Turks were abandoning their positions and withdrawing to the East. Seaplane reconnaissance continued to paint the picture for the British command that the Turks were reinforcing in Beersheba and Maxwell braced for another attack. But the attack never came. The Turks, like the British, had shifted their operational focus to the Gallipoli Peninsula. As the interest in the Suez waned on both sides, resources were diverted to assist in other flashpoints of the war. A large part of the British troops from Egypt were sent to Gallipoli, while the RFC detachment remained at Ismailia. This detachment departed for Mesopotamia in October to join two flights that were already operating there as part of No. 30 Squadron.[25]

Egypt did not go without aircraft for very long. In November 1915, Fifth wing was established in Egypt under the command of the very able Lieutenant-Colonel W.G.H. Salmond, who took over responsibility of all airplane cooperation in theater. The Fifth wing was made up of No. 14 and No. 17 Squadrons as well as "X" Aircraft Park. The Wing headquarters was initially established at Heliopolis, while the "X" Aircraft Park was placed in a former Swiss Iron Foundry at Abbassia--located between Heliopolis and Cairo.[26]

By the time that the Fifth Wing had arrived in Egypt, Turkey and her allies had developed threats towards the British position on the Suez from three different directions. The first threat came from the Turkish forces mobilizing and consolidating at Beersheba for an attack against the canal. The second threat was from the unrest that was brewing in the Sudan, where the Sultan of Darfur was threatening to attack Kordofan. And the third threat was from the growing tribe of Bedouin, called the Senussi, that was rising in the desert West of Cairo. These Senussi had been infiltrated by Turkish and German agents over the past year and were persuaded to initiate a Jihad against all of Turkey's enemies-- which included the British outposts West of Cairo.[27] The Fifth wing spent the rest of 1915 in support of British operations against the Senussi in the Western Egyptian desert and against the forces of Darfur.

In December 1915, Maxwell decided to push his defenses out to the East of the canal to protect the canal zone from artillery fire. This required tremendous preparations. Once the British abandoned their operations on the Gallipoli Peninsula, their attention turned once again to the defense of the Suez Canal. In January 1916, British troops were sent directly from the Dardanelles to Egypt. At this time, Lieutenant-General Sir Archibald Murray was appointed to the command of the Mediterranean Expeditionary group responsible for the defense of the Suez Canal. Meanwhile, Lieutenant-General Maxell remained in "general command in Egypt with responsibility for the defense of the Western Frontier."[28] This was an awkward arrangement at best, and by 10 March 1916 Sir John Maxwell returned to Britain and Sir Archibald Murray assumed command of all of Egypt.[29]

In February 1916, Lieutenant-Colonel Salmond collocated the Fifth Wing Headquarters with Murray's headquarters at Ismailia. Salmond initiated a series of lectures at Ismailia to military officers in order to explain the organization, capabilities and combined-arms effects of the Royal Flying Corps. The main duty of the RFC during the first few months of 1916 was to conduct reconnaissance duties in cooperation with the Topographical Section of the Intelligence Branch. This greatly improved the accuracy of aerial reconnaissance reports.

In April 1916 the tables began to turn for the Palestinian theater as the first German aeroplanes were seen over the Sinai. The German Rumpler and Fokker E-I fighters quickly gained a technical superiority over the British and retained it until the autumn of the next year. A new phase was emerging, one in which the British would have to fight for the information that until now had been readily available. Furthermore, the British would have to fight off the German observers.

Summary

The small force that the British sent to defend the Suez Canal towards the end of 1914, succeeded because it possessed the capability to conduct aerial reconnaissance. Although they were outnumbered, the British were able to concentrate their forces effectively due to the information they gained from aerial reconnaissance. The British managed to maintain their dominance in the air throughout 1915 simply because there was no air threat opposing them in the theater. The end of this phase, February 1916, was a period of transition.

The British managed to stave off two attacks on the canal by early 1916, when the First Lord of the Admiralty, Winston Churchill, argued that the British should attempt a more indirect approach to the war. The Egyptian Expeditionary Force (EEF) was born. The intent behind the British efforts in the middle-east was to defeat the Turkish forces; remove the Ottoman Empire from the war; and threaten the German-Austrian territories from the Balkans.[30]

New British leadership and German aircraft were being introduced into the theater. This fact was indicative of the change, change in the dynamics of the theater as well as in the strategy of the war effort. By early 1916, Germany was beginning to produce better aircraft and in sufficient quantities to proliferate all theaters of the war. The aircraft the Germans sent to Palestine were some of the best of their time. The Palestine Brigade of the Royal Flying Corps was no longer alone in the air over the Sinai. And the German pilots were quite unwelcomed company.

This first phase set the stage for the RFC in this theater. The RFC in Egypt was an integral part of the British force. Under the direction of Salmond, the importance, relevance and capabilities of the RFC continued to develop throughout the war in this theater. Salmond provided not only the direction and energy for the RFC in Egypt, but he was also the source of continuity throughout the three phases of operations in Palestine.

---

[1]John Bourne, *Sir John Grenfell Maxwell (1859-1929)* (Available from: http://www. firstworldwar.bham.ac.uk/donkey/maxwell.htm, accessed 28 February 2007), 1.

[2]Michael Duffy, *Who's Who: Sir John Maxwell* (Available from: http://www. firstworldwar.com/bio/maxwell_john.htm, accessed 13 February 2007), 1.

[3]H.A. Jones, *The War in the Air*, Vol. 5 (Oxford: Clarendon Press, 1935), 160.

[4]Ibid.

[5]Ibid., 161.

[6]Baker, A., 12.

[7]Ibid., 23.

[8]Ibid., 24.

[9]Ibid., 62.

[10]Ibid., 67.

[11]Ibid., 68.

[12]Ibid., 79.

[13]Jones, *The War in the Air*, Vol. 5, 178.

[14]Ibid., 179.

[15]Baker, A., 20.

[16]Jones, *The War in the Air*, Vol. 5, 163.

[17]Ibid., 167.

[18]Ibid., 178.

[19]Baker, A., 86.

[20]Jones, *The War in the Air*, Vol. 5, 166.

[21]Ibid., 165.

[22]Ibid., 161.

[23]Ibid., 163.

[24]Ibid.

[25]Ibid., 166.

[26]Ibid., 165.

[27]Baker, A., 81.

[28]Jones, *The War in the Air*, Vol. 5, 177.

[29]Ibid., 178.

[30]Baker, A., 106.

CHAPTER 3

PHASE II: MARCH 1916 TO APRIL 1917

This phase of operations in Egypt and Palestine was a period of transition. The Allied Forces in this theater transitioned from the defense to the offense, while the Turks abandoned their attempts to seize the Suez Canal and transitioned to the defense of the Gaza Beersheba line in lower Palestine. In the meantime, The Royal Flying Corps in Egypt was now facing opposition in the air for the first time in the war. The RFC was woefully outmatched in the quality of aircraft compared to the German Air Service in Palestine, and did not receive aircraft to effectively oppose the Germans until the end of this phase.

As a result, the RFC focused on the development of pilot training and innovations to improve all facets of their support role. This transition served to strengthen the structure of the RFC, improve the quality of its pilots, and provide broader and more effective support to the EEF's offensive operations. Although this phase was marked with two failed attempts to seize Gaza, these failures served as the catalyst for change, improvement and victory. Specifically, the German Air Service's uncontested aerial reconnaissance of Allied dispositions provided the Turkish defense of Gaza the same edge that the Allies enjoyed during their defense of the Suez Canal. By the end of this phase the RFC learned the dual nature of their role, to deny the enemy's aerial reconnaissance abilities while exploiting their own.

Leadership

Commander, Mediterranean Expeditionary Force, Lieutenant-General Sir Archibald Murray

One of the most significant changes during this phase of operations in Egypt and Palestine was Lieutenant-General Murray's assumption of command. His presence brought with it a fresh perspective and an enthusiasm for offensive operations. He was out to prove himself.

Archibald Murray was in command of a division when war broke out in August 1914. He relinquished this post when he was offered the position of Chief of Staff to General Sir John French and the original British Expeditionary Force. Murray was an "unhappy" choice however.[1] The position was originally earmarked for Sir Henry Wilson, but Wilson was deemed politically unacceptable after the "Curragh Mutiny," an incident that took place on 20 July 1914, in County Kildare, Ireland. Murray's appointment as French's Chief of Staff was a recipe for failure.

Most of Murray's subordinate staff officers had worked closely with Sir Henry Wilson at the War Office's Directorate of Military Operations. The commander and chief, General French, was also a close personal friend of Wilson and openly admitted to his "preference of Wilson's company and advice."[2] Murray's position was further complicated by Wilson himself, who remained at the General Headquarters as MGGS, and made every attempt to undermine Murray's authority.

Despite the difficulty of his position, Murray is solely to blame for being unable to overcome the situation through demonstration of ability, strength of will or force of character. He was replaced in January 1915 by Sir William Robertson and was appointed as Deputy and then Chief of the Imperial General Staff (CIGS). He was again replaced by

Sir William Robertson in December 1915, and in January 1916, Murray was offered command of the British forces in Egypt, which he renamed as the Egyptian Expeditionary Force, or EEF.[3]

Murray was enthusiastic about his new command. It was a post in which he was able to exercise his ideas with a certain amount of autonomy and without being undermined at every turn. Murray received guidance from General Robertson, as the CIGS, who emphasized to him that France was Britain's primary theater. He also received guidance from Lord Kitchener, the Secretary of State for War, who told him that he must "maintain as active a defense as possible" in order to prevent the Turks from ranging the canal zone with artillery.[4] As a result, Murray made the decision to extend his defenses east of the canal by about 11,000 yards. He established a formidable defense of the canal zone which comprised of two lines of defensive trench works as well as fortified bridgeheads at the canal.

Almost as soon as he took command, Sir Archibald Murray stressed the importance of an air photographic survey. He stressed the cooperation between the aerial observers and the Topographical section of the Intelligence Branch. The two organizations working together were able to develop pin-point reference systems in which even the most featureless areas of the desert where identifiable. There was extensive aerial photography taken of the canal zone during this period and the photographs were transferred to 1:20,000 squared maps. This technique was a further development of the system Lieutenant Colonel Salmond had devised in France.[5]

Once the canal zone defenses were complete, Murray made the decision to cross the Sinai. Whether it was out of his desire to stir his men out of the complacency of static

43

defense or out of the desire to vindicate himself with an impressive victory over the Turks, we will never know. However, crossing the Sinai with an army was a logistical nightmare. Murray decided to initiate the construction of a rail and water-pipe system across the Sinai to sustain his forces as they marched across. This effort was undertaken mostly by the Egyptian Labour Corps (ELC) and its offspring the Camel Transport Corps (CTC).[6] This force of Egyptian laborers were employed in digging trenches, laying railway lines and water pipes in order to spare the British soldiers of this back-breaking mundane work--so that they could be prepared to fight. In the process the ELC and CTC laid the foundation for the future success of the Egyptian Expeditionary Force with their bare hands. Despite whatever criticism might be leveled against Sir Archibald Murray, his defensive preparations and logistic infrastructure in Egypt were great achievements upon which any future British successes would depend.

Commander, Middle East Brigade, RFC, Brigadier General Geoffrey Salmond

On 1 July 1916, Geoffrey Salmond was promoted to Brigadier General and given command of the Middle East Brigade. The Brigade consolidated all detachments located in Egypt, Mesopotamia, East Africa and, later, Salonika under one command. In addition to this, Brigadier General Salmond received permission to form the Twentieth Reserve Wing. This wing was to consist of three squadrons--the 21, 22, and 23 Squadrons, as well as an aircraft park and depot.[7] The squadrons, park and depot were due to arrive between June and September and would be located at Abukir, Egypt. The purpose of this wing was to train pilots for the Middle East Brigade and also to serve as a general training establishment for the RFC.

Equipment

British Aeroplanes

For most of this phase of operations in Egypt and Palestine, the RFC was operating the same equipment it had since the end of 1915. The majority of the aircraft in the RFC were reconnaissance platforms until late in 1916, when the RFC received both Martinsyde Bombers and DH2 fighters. (See Appendix B). Upon receipt of the DH2 fighters the RFC in Egypt designated its first single-seat fighter squadron, Number 24 Squadron. The significance of this disparity of aircraft quality on the part of the RFC during this phase meant that they had to adapt. Adaptation takes cunning and ingenuity. During this phase, the RFC improved upon what it had by increasing wireless communication capabilities, artillery spotting techniques and piloting skills (mostly to avoid the German fighters).

German Aeroplanes

During early 1916, the Germans introduced their newest fighter, the Fokker Eindecker E-I. This monoplane was responsible for the period known as the "Fokker Scourge" in which the German fighters dominated the skies over the Western Front. The Fokkers had a similar effect over the skies of Palestine. This aircraft utilized a synchronization gear which caused the forward firing machine gun to pause when the propeller blade was directly in front of the barrel, thus it allowed the pilot fire forward. It was one of the first dedicated fighters developed in the war and its introduction caught the Allies unprepared to challenge, and caused them to feverishly work to develop a cure for the "Fokker Scourge."

The Germans had made some impressive aircraft developments in 1916, but none that surpassed the edge they obtained with the production of the Fokker eindeckers. By the Spring of 1917, the Albatross fighters were dominating the scene on the Western Front. But these aircraft did not see service in the Palestine theater. From 1916 to 1917, the German pilots flying in support of the Yilderim were flying mostly Rumpler C-I and Fokker eindeckers.

Training and Tactics

The Training Brigade in Egypt

During the Spring and Summer of 1916 there was a great deal of activity in the RFC. Due to the quickly developing technologies in the aviation industry as well as the toll that the German Fokkers were having on the British aeroplanes, the RFC had to begin to produce not only a better quality of pilot but also a quantity that would outpace the casualty rate among pilots. Salmond realized how ideal the conditions were in Egypt for flight training. Flight training depended so greatly on the weather, which in Britain was mostly adverse towards training. Salmond noticed that in Egypt, there was hardly a time that the aeroplanes were grounded due to adverse weather.

Geoffrey Salmond wrote to General Henderson, his former boss, suggesting that Egypt's good weather and climate would be an ideal training ground for pilots of the RFC. His notion was supported by General Trenchard and soon after by the British Government.[8] It was an ambitious undertaking; but Geoffrey Salmond was an ambitious man.

In response to the ideas suggested by Lieutenant Colonel Salmond in the early Spring of 1916, the War Office decided to organize a training establishment for pilots in

Egypt. The intent for this training organization was to have one hundred pilots under instruction at a time. In order to accomplish this, three reserve squadrons would be needed. The personnel were dispatched to Egypt in July 1916, and the three squadrons were formed: No. 21 was organized at Abassia on 12 July, while Nos. 22 and 23 were established at Abu Qir on 24 August. These three reserve squadrons were grouped together to form the Twentieth Reserve Wing on 15 September under the command of Lieutenant Colonel A.G. Board.[9] The students entered No 21 Squadron for elementary flight training, passed into No. 22 Squadron for intermediate training, and into No. 23 Squadron for advanced tactical training and graduation. Some of these students returned to Britain after 15 hours of solo time, while the rest filled flying positions within the Middle East Brigade.[10]

Another type of innovation was being carried out in the Training Brigade--training for noncommissioned officers and mechanics. The No. 3 School of Military Aeronautics, officially formed in November 1916, but actually began as early as August in a back room of the officer's mess. Lectures and practical exercises were carried out on subjects ranging from engines to rigging. The first examination was given in September 1916. In December 1916, a fourth Squadron was added to the Twentieth Reserve Wing---57 Squadron, formed at Ismailia from personnel trained by the Fifth Wing. The official history of the air war comments that "as a result of the efficient training organization in Egypt, the Middle East Brigade came to be not only self-dependent, but it also was able to supply trained pilots for other theaters of war."[11]

Due to the expansion of the brigade as a whole, even the small functions that had developed over the past year were amplified. "A small training class grew into a school of aerial gunnery; from another class there developed a school of military aeronautics; and separate schools came to be established for instruction in artillery co-operation and in bombing."[12] All this instruction in addition to the cadet wing (Twentieth Reserve Wing) provided a rich exchange of ideas within the brigade. Furthermore, the growth of these organizations required temporary as well as semi-permanent facilities. The Middle East Brigade had its own engineer for these projects and he managed a large force of native laborers. This group constructed aerodromes, hangars, depots, and repair centers.

<u>Organization and Operations</u>

Australian Flying Corps arrives in Egypt

At the end of 1915, the Army council had suggested that the Dominions should raise squadrons for the Royal Flying Corps. Australia accepted the challenge and formed the No 1. Australian Flying Corps. This force consisted of 28 officers, 195 other ranks but no aeroplanes or technical equipment. They departed Melbourne on 16 March 1916, and arrived at the Suez on 14 April.[13] It took approximately six weeks to outfit the No. 1 AFC Squadron with aeroplanes and equipment. They received mostly B.E.2a and B.E.2c aircraft.[14] By 1916, these variants were already outdated and underpowered. To the credit of Australian Flying Corps, they were able to make do with the machines and even innovate with them.

A young Lieutenant named L.J. Wackett was particularly inventive. He devised an arrangement for a Lewis gun to mount on the top wing of his B.E.2c. This gave two German Rumplers quite a surprise when, while being pursued by them, he turned on them and fired--the Rumplers disengaged. He also created a system in which he could sling and drop canisters from underneath his aircraft. Later in the war, this device allowed 1st

Squadron the ability to deliver over 100,000 rounds of ammunition to Monash's advancing machine gunners.[15]

By the end of 1916, the AFC No. 1 Squadron received Bristol Scouts as fighter escorts. Two AFC pilots, Lieutenants W.J. Weir and Carrick S. Paul, painted their plane bright yellow. As such, they earned a reputation among their own squadron as well as among the Turks. Their success led the Turks to order: "All ranks are to take immediate cover on approach of the yellow English airplane." Lieutenant Weir would become one of the few aces in the Palestine theater of operations.[16]

Development of the Middle East Brigade

As mentioned previously, the Middle East Brigade was formed on 1 July 1916, under the command of the newly promoted Brigadier General W. G. H. Salmond. With its headquarters at Ismailia (see figure 6), the brigade consisted of No. 14 and 17 Squadrons of the RFC and No.1 Squadron of the AFC, as well as the Twentieth Reserve Wing (consisting of Nos. 21, 22, and 23 Squadrons), the "X" Aircraft Park, and "X" Aircraft Depot, all in Egypt; In addition to these, the Brigade had the No. 30 Squadron and Aircraft park in Mesopotamia and the No. 26 Squadron and Aircraft Park in East Africa. This Brigade was responsible for the administration, organization and maintenance of all RFC detachments in the Middle East.[17]

The formation of this brigade created an increased personnel requirement to satisfy the demands of its rapidly expanding role and responsibility. Most of these personnel were obtained by "combing through the armies in the four theaters of war."[18] As a result, many of the officers and men of the Middle East Brigade had served in all theaters of the Middle East, either on the ground or in the air. Therefore, many of the squadrons were representative of the whole brigade. This coupled with the organization and expansion of training establishments in Egypt, gave the Brigade a reputation for capability and innovation.

The Middle East Brigade Headquarters was called upon at times to develop solutions for unprecedented problems as the War Office struggled to develop new tactics to suit the rapidly changing conditions of the war. In this way, the Brigade Headquarters "constituted a clearing house for ideas."[19] The Middle East Brigade Staff studied operations in all theaters of the war and communicated ideas between the theaters regarding the successes or failures of tactics and techniques.[20]

Defense of Suez in August 1916: the Battle of Romani

From the end of June to the middle of July 1916, air reconnaissance reported a considerable growth in activity at the Turkish camp of Bir el Mazar, located approximately forty-two miles from Romani (see figure 6). These reports coupled with reports from agents that warned of a Turkish advance on Qatiya--a British outpost. But the British command grew doubtful whether the attack was imminent and was inclined to believe that the campaigning season was over, and that the Turks would probably wait until winter. On 19 July, air reconnaissance confirmed the presence of approximately 8,000 Turkish troops with camel transport moving west from Bir el Mazar. The offensive was on.[21]

The British General Staff adopted a strategy of allowing the Turks to proceed with their attack against British prepared positions in order to facilitate a British envelopment and counter-attack. Therefore, the Royal Flying Corps did not harass the advancing Turks, but continued to provide reports of their positions. Brigadier-General Salmond issued orders on 1 August 1916, detailing the cooperation plan for the RFC and

51

AFC squadrons from Qantara to directly coordinate with the British 52nd Division and the Anzac Mounted Division located at Romani.[22] The Turks initiated their bold attack on the night of 3 August and the battle raged until the next evening. During the fight, pilots from the Middle East Brigade flew daring missions to interdict, report and direct artillery fires. In one instance, an aerial observer directed artillery for over an hour on the Turkish camp at Hod um Ugba, in which four direct hits were achieved.[23]

The British advance began on the morning of 5 August as the Turks pounded a retreat. The Turks did attempt to make a stand at Oghratina (half-way between Romani and Bir el Mazar) (see Figure 5) on 6 August, but this melted away after two days. By 13 August, the British occupied Salmana and the Turks retreated to El Arish. The Turks lost approximately 4,000 troops as prisoners, while the British suffered 1,130 casualties (202 of which were killed). The RFC had flown all available aeroplanes in support of the battle, which consisted of approximately seventeen aircraft, with the pilots flying an average of three missions per day while the fighting persisted.[24]

Advance into Palestine

Cavalry Raid on Bir El Mazar

After the attack on the Suez canal was thwarted in August 1916, the Turks withdrew but left an outpost force at Bir el Mazar. Despite their Turks' loss, however, the German pilots did not relent their air attacks and continued to be aggressive. They attacked Port Said on 1 September and inflicted 46 casualties, also dropping bombs on the carrier *Raven II*--which caused considerable damage to the ship and prevented its expedition to the Red Sea.[25]

A British force was assembled at Salmana on 16 September with the mission of carrying out a cavalry raid on the Turkish garrison at Bir el Mazar. In support of this operation the RFC was instructed to prevent German aircraft from making reconnaissance over Salmana. This was critical to the raid, since its success would hinge on surprise and the location of Salmana, with its scattering of palm groves, offered very little cover for the British force. So the RFC carried out an attack on the German aerodrome at El Arish on 15 and 16 September, while simultaneously arranging air patrols to intercept any enemy planes that attempted to reconnoiter Salmana.[26]

The bombing mission on El Arish was defeated by German Fokker intercept fighters and the air patrol did not succeed in holding off the enemy reconnaissance efforts. On the 16 September, a German pilot slipped through an unprotected corridor to Salmana and discovered the cavalry formation. The German proceeded to bomb the formations, without affect. But the hope for surprise was lost. Nonetheless, the Cavalry raid proceeded at dawn on 17 September and found the Turks well positioned and prepared for the assault. After a brief skirmish, the attack was called off.[27] This action, while a failed one, taught an important lesson to the cavalry as well as the RFC. In the sparse desert landscape, air superiority was absolutely essential in denying the enemy knowledge of an impending offensive action. This lesson would be heeded and enacted two years later in Palestine.

1st Battle of Gaza

By March 1917, Sir Archibald Murray had advanced across the Sinai, inching his way from outpost to outpost while constructing railways and water pipelines in his wake. He had succeeded in wrestling Magdhaba and Rafah from the Turks and decided that it

53

was time to attack along the coast to Gaza. The operation was to be conducted by the Eastern Force, which consisted of the Desert Column (ANZAC Mounted Division, Imperial Mounted Division, and 53rd Division), The Imperial Camel Brigade, 52nd and 54th Divisions, as well as the 229th Brigade of the 74th Division. The Desert Column was to lead the attack with the rest of the Eastern Force in support and prepared to exploit success. Two flights from the No. 67th Squadron (Formerly the No. 1 Australian Squadron) were sent forward to the aerodrome at Rafah to provide support for the offensive. The rest of Fifth Wing operated out of Ramah during the battle but returned to their aerodromes each night.

The attack was launched on 26 March 1917. In support of the Eastern Force, the Fifth Wing Commander, Lieutenant-Colonel Borton, issued an operation order in which the wing would maintain a constant presence of a contact patrol with the Desert Column, while five aeroplanes conducted reconnaissance missions, six aeroplanes detailed for artillery cooperation, and six aeroplanes detailed for patrol duties.[28]

In the early part March, the Turkish force consisted of: two battalions and two batteries defending Gaza; the Turkish 16th Division positioned fifteen miles south-east of Gaza; the Turkish 3rd Division in reserve eleven miles east of Gaza; and a Cavalry Brigade with one regiment of the 27th Arab Division at Beersheba. But this force was supported by the German air service which was able to out-distance the aeroplanes of the RFC. The German pilots were able to fly daily reconnaissance missions over British camps and report on their activities and disposition.[29] These reports gave the Turks a clear indication of the British intention to attack Gaza. In response, the commander of the Turkish formations, Kress, strengthened the defenses at Gaza with additional artillery, as well as parts of the Turkish 16th and 53rd Divisions. All this action increased the size of the Turkish force defending Gaza a total of seven battalions and several artillery batteries.

At the beginning of the attack on 26 March, the German aeroplanes once again provided timely reports to the Turkish defenders, reporting that "strong British forces were advancing on Gaza from the South."[30] With this report, Kress maneuvered his remaining forces to reinforce Gaza as well as attack the British rear area. He ordered the force in Gaza to defend to the last man. By 11 a.m. British mounted troops had completely surrounded Gaza, but the Eastern Force Commander, Lieutenant-General Dobell believed his position was tenuous. He believed that the Turks were amassing a strong counter-attack force which would be put against his vulnerable right-rear flank. Dobell issued orders to withdraw on the evening of 26 March and the withdrawal continued until 28 March, when the Eastern Force took up a position on the south bank of the Wadi Ghazze.[31] The failure of the attack was complete.

The British suffered 4,000 casualties (523 killed) in the three day attack, and the Turks suffered 2,447 casualties (301 killed and 1,061 missing).[32] In the end, it was evident that the German air service had contributed immensely to the success of the Turks in repulsing the attack. The German Rumplers were able to outrun the British aeroplanes and therefore avoid air combat in order to conduct reconnaissance, while the German Halberstadt fighters sought every opportunity to attack the British pilots. Overall, the RFC was unable to deny the enemy its aerial reconnaissance capability. This reconnaissance capability was essential to the Turkish defense.[33]

<u>2nd Battle of Gaza</u>

The guidance that Sir Archibald Murray received prior to his attack on Gaza was that the intent of the operations in Palestine was to put pressure on the enemy there in order to help the Spring offenses on other fronts.[34] After his first attack on Gaza failed, he received a telegram on 30 March 1917 directing him to attack and defeat the Turks south of Jerusalem and to take the city immediately. Lloyd George, who assumed the position of Prime Minister in December 1916, was resolute in his strategy of attacking the Central Powers where they were weakest--Turkey. Knocking Turkey out of the war would expose Germany to an attack from the rear, while she was entrenched in the war in France.[35]

This second attack, however, would have virtually no possibility of surprise. Since the Turks now occupied Gaza in force and had dug in, any plan for attack on Gaza would be a siege in which artillery would play the decisive role. However, the careful planning and preparation required to conduct such an attack would also allow the enemy more time to fortify and strengthen his defenses.

The plan for the attack against Gaza was a frontal assault on the city with three divisions. The attack was to have two phases. The first phase was an advance up to attack positions located just beyond the Wadi Ghazze. The divisions would consolidate in their attack positions and prepare for the assault. During this pause, which was to last one full day, the city and defensive positions would be subjected to a heavy artillery bombardment from land as well as sea. Then the second phase would be initiated, in which the Eastern Force Commanding General would direct the attack against the city, free to exploit success wherever it occurred. Upon capturing the city, two divisions would defend to the North and East while one division entered and cleared the city.

The first phase was launched on 17 April 1917 and was mostly uneventful. The British artillery bombarded the Turkish positions on 18 April and the second phase was launched on 19 April. Despite the tenacity and gallantry of the British, the force lacked sufficient artillery and ammunition to break through the defended positions. By the evening of 19 April, it was evident to the Eastern Force Commander that the attack would not be successful. The British forces consolidated in a line north of the Wadi Ghazze. The British lost approximately 500 men in the attack and the Turks lost 400 killed.[36]

The Royal Flying Corps conducted important operations in support of the second attack on Gaza. Prior to the battle, the RFC conducted extensive tactical and strategic reconnaissance. The photos that the RFC provided resulted in a new 1:40,000 map that was produced and printed in time for the initiation of operations. During the attack, the RFC conducted artillery cooperation, making thirty-eight flights in two days engaging sixty-three targets, of which twenty-seven were enemy batteries. Also important to note is that a reconnaissance flight on 20 April 1916, identified approximately 2,000 infantry and 800 cavalry assembled for an apparent counterattack against the British right flank. Four aeroplanes were dispatched to interdict. They conducted ground attacks against the Turkish formations which caused them to scatter. The counter-attack never materialized.[37]

<u>Summary</u>

While this phase of operations in Egypt and Palestine are marked with several failures, there were many successes and lessons that the British gleaned from their experiences. First, Murray succeeded in thwarting the Turkish attacks against the Suez Canal so successfully that the Turks abandoned their effort against it. Furthermore, his series of counter-attacks drove the Turks across the Sinai towards Gaza. In his wake, Murray successfully established critical logistic nodes and a fresh water pipeline across the Northern coast of the Sinai. These actions set the conditions for success in the next phase, upon which Allenby capitalized.

As far as the RFC Palestine Brigade is concerned, this phase, although marred in failures, was their springboard to success. As a result of the German Air Service's successful aerial reconnaissance efforts, the Turks were able to mount effective defenses at Bir El Mazar and Gaza. In the sparse desert terrain it is difficult to mask movements of large forces to achieve surprise. It is especially difficult to conceal these movements from aerial observation. The Palestine Brigade learned that their foremost mission in support of the ground forces was to deny the enemy aerial reconnaissance. To accomplish this task it was absolutely essential that the RFC possess the right equipment, specifically fighters, that were superior or at least comparable to those of the German Air Service. The failures of the EEF at Gaza caught the attention of the British War Ministry. The RFC would get everything they requested and more.

Although the RFC Palestine Brigade was outclassed by the German aircraft, there was an important edge that the brigade was honing. By the end of this phase, the Palestine Brigade was churning out a good volume of trained pilots and mechanics, approximately 100 pilots per month average.[38] As a result, the RFC was generating a pilot to plane ratio that was far exceeding that of the German Air Service. The quality of the British pilots was also improving as a result of professional dialogue and training methods within the RFC. In contrast, the German Air Service in Palestine was having difficulty maintaining a steady flow of trained pilots. Furthermore, disease and poor medical conditions was slowly eroding the pool of pilots that were available to the Germans. Machines themselves are nothing without capable operators.

Finally, although the Germans had a technological edge over the British in Egypt, they failed to fully capitalize on it. They neither sought to destroy the British aerodromes in Egypt, nor did they fully integrate their efforts with the Turkish ground forces. Instead, they acted independently, providing good reconnaissance of the British lines and harassing the British reconnaissance efforts. But they did not act decisively to destroy the RFC in Palestine.

---

[1]J.M. Bourne, *Who's Who in World War One* (London: Routledge, 2001).

[2]Ibid.

[3]David R. Woodward, *Hell in the Holy Land: World War I in the Middle East* (Lexington: University Press of Kentucky, 2006), 20.

[4]Ibid., 20.

[5]Baker, A., 85.

[6]Woodward, 36.

[7]Jones, *War in the Air*, vol.5, 449.

[8]Baker, A., 88.

[9]Jones, *War in the Air*, vol.5, 449.

[10]Ibid., 450.

[11]Ibid., 188.

[12]Ibid..

[13]F. M. Cutlack, *The Official History of Australia in the War of 1914-1918*, vol. 7, *The Australian Flying Corps,* ed. Robert O'Neill (St. Lucia, Queensland: University of Queensland Press, 1923), 33.

[14]Ibid., 31-33.

[15]Cameron Riley, *The Australian Flying Corps 1914-1919* (Available from: www.australianflyingcorps.org/2002_1999/afc_about.htm, accessed 18 March 2007).

[16]Ibid.

[17]Jones, *War in the Air*, vol.5, 189.

[18]Ibid., 188.

[19]Ibid.

[20]Ibid., 189.

[21]Ibid., 192.

[22]Ibid., 193.

[23]Ibid., 194.

[24]Ibid.

[25]Ibid., 196.

[26]Ibid.

[27]Ibid., 197.

[28]Ibid., 209.

[29]Ibid., 210.

[30]Ibid.

[31]Ibid., 213.

[32]Ibid., 214.

[33]Ibid.

[34]Ibid., 215.

[35]Baker, A., 106.

[36]Jones, *War in the Air*, vol.5, 217.

[37]Ibid.

[38]Ibid., 451.

CHAPTER 4

PHASE III: APRIL 1917 TO NOVEMBER 1918

This phase of operations in Palestine was a period of culmination. By the time

Allenby arrived in theater, the EEF as well as the RFC Palestine Brigade were already

sewing the seeds for future success. The EEF was establishing vital logistic nodes across

the Northern Sinai and assisting the Arab Northern Army in their operations East of the

Jordan River. The RFC was providing very well trained pilots and was continuing to

hone the innovations that it had made in the way of artillery spotting techniques and air-

to-ground communications.

While this phase began with the German Air Service dominating the skies in

virtually all theaters of the war, it ended in their ultimate defeat in the air as well as on the

ground. As an organization, the RFC Palestine Brigade learned valuable lessons from the

first two phases of operations in Egypt and Palestine. Specifically, they learned the

importance of aerial reconnaissance in defensive operations. If there was to be any hope

for success on the ground, the RFC needed to ensure two things: that the enemy was

denied the ability to conduct aerial reconnaissance, and that the RFC maintained routine,

rapid and accurate reporting of enemy positions and friendly progress.

The quality of leadership, training, equipment and planning culminated in this

phase of operations in Palestine. The RFC as well as the EEF capitalized on the

evolutionary development and maturation of infrastructure and personnel in this phase,

while Allenby provided the impetus, direction and energy for success.

Leadership

Commander, Egyptian Expeditionary Force
General Sir Edmund H. H. Allenby

Edmund Henry Hynman Allenby was born in Brackenhurst, Nottinghamshire, Britain in 1861. He was educated at Haileybury College and graduated from the Royal Military College, Sandhurst in 1881. He was commissioned in the 6th Inniskilling Dragoons and served in South Africa from 1884-1885. He attended Staff College in Camberley in 1894 along with Captain Douglas Haig of the 7th Hussars; it was there that the two officers initiated a personal rivalry that lasted through to the First World War.

Allenby graduated Staff college in 1897 and returned to South Africa at the outbreak of the Boer War in 1899. While there, Allenby served as second in command of the Inniskillings and was given command of a cavalry squadron in which capacity he excelled. In April 1900, he was given temporary command of the Inniskillings when the commander was wounded and returned to Britain. Allenby served in the Boer War with distinction until the war's end in 1902, capturing the attention of both Lords Roberts and Kitchener.

When the war broke out in 1914, Allenby was made commander of a Cavalry Division in the British Expeditionary Force. After his skillful covering force actions following the BEF's retreat from the Battle of Mons, Allenby was promoted to GOC Cavalry Corps, V Corps. In April and May 1917, Allenby commanded Third Army at the Battle of Arras. In terms of casualties suffered per day, Arras was the costliest British battle of the war. The battle began well, but his advance soon halted and met stiffening German resistance. As the casualties began to mount, several of Allenby's subordinate commanders voiced their protests to Field Marshall Haig. Allenby was relieved of command on 9 June 1917 and replaced by Julian Byng. While Allenby regarded the relief to be the result of his failure at Arras as well as his tactical arguments with Haig, he didn't realize that there were other forces at work.

After the failure of the second attack on Gaza, Lloyd George pressed the War Department for a successor to Sir Archibald Murray. General Robertson suggested Sir Edmund Allenby, Lord Kitchener and Sir John French gave their support for the recommendation. When Allenby arrived in London and conferred with Lloyd George he was inspired by the Prime Minister's enthusiasm. The Prime Minister explained to Allenby that he would have freedom of action to conduct his campaigns as he saw fit and that he was to ask for all the reinforcements and supplies that he might need. But there was a price. Lloyd George demanded of Allenby that he "take Jerusalem by Christmas."[1]

General Sir Edmund Allenby took over command of the Egyptian Expeditionary Force in Cairo on 28 June 1917. At once, his mere presence had begun to change the attitude and atmosphere of the force. The arrival of Allenby in Egypt was most eloquently stated by T. E. Lawrence: "Allenby's coming had re-made the English. His breadth of personality swept away the mist of private or departmental jealousies behind which Murray and his men had worked."[2]

Commander, Middle East Brigade, Royal Air Force (1 April 1918),
Major-General Sir Geoffrey Salmond

With the arrival of Allenby in Cairo in June 1917, there was a palpable change in the atmosphere of the Egyptian Expeditionary Force. The men of the EEF, including

Salmond, savored it. His arrival also brought great changes for the Middle East Brigade.

Salmond received a telegram while on leave in Britain in July 1917 which read:

> To G.O.C. Middle East Brigade, Egypt. 10/7/17. It has been decided to raise a fighter squadron in Egypt, the officers, pilots and personnel to be found locally so far as possible. Squadron equipment will be sent from England. No further allotment of aeroplanes will be made at present beyond those already allocated at the beginning of this month, nor will any definite type of machine be laid down at present, but for the next two or three months it is assumed that this equipment will consist partly of Bristol Fighters, Bristol Monoplanes and Vickers Bullets. If assistance is absolutely necessary in personnel, please cable particulars of minimum requirements. The Squadron will be designated No. 111.[3]

At last, a fighter squadron in Egypt! Shortly after his return to Egypt, Salmond received word from the War office that another squadron, No. 113, was to be raised in Egypt at Ismailia. It was Allenby that ordered the Bristol Fighters for Egypt. Allenby was a cavalry man and witnessed first-hand the importance of aeroplanes in conducting reconnaissance and of the fighter aircraft in conducting counter-reconnaissance. Allenby wanted to wrestle the enemy's eyes from the skies, and with the promise of a new fighter squadron, Salmond would be happy to do it.

As preparations were being made in October 1917 for the attack into Palestine, Brigadier General Salmond received word that he was being sent back to Britain. German Gothas carried out a daylight raid on London on 7 July 1917. They killed fifty-seven people in the process, and the event led to a public outcry regarding British air defense preparedness. In reaction to the attack, the British Government initiated a series of sweeping decisions to examine the reshuffling of the British Air Organizations and the direction of Air Operations. Much to his disappointment, Salmond was being summoned home to be part of the process of remodeling the RFC.[4] These were the birth pangs of the Royal Air Force.

As Salmond awaited transport in Cairo bound for Britain, he received a hand written letter from Allenby, who was on the move towards Jerusalem. It read:

> GHQ Egyptian Expeditionary Force: My dear Salmond, I hear that you are still in Cairo, stopped by the congestion on the Italian railways. I take the opportunity to write and thank you for the splendid work of organization and training you carried out while you were here. Its results are shown in the mastery of the air which our flying men have attained. Their exploits have been wonderful--nothing stops them--in fighting or reconnaissance. We have won a great victory; I wish you were with us, to take part in the success you have done so much to ensure. It must be galling you to have missed it. I wish you the best of good fortune, and am your gratefully and sincerely."[5]

And so, while the Middle East Brigade fought to control the skies over the successfully advancing EEF, Salmond returned to London. He was not present for Allenby's victories at Beersheba nor for his triumphant march into Jerusalem. But Allenby did not forget the man who was a key to his success.

After his victory in Jerusalem in December 1917, Allenby recommended to the War Office that the RFC command in the Middle Eastern Theater be reorganized. Since the service had been greatly expanded, Allenby recommended that the RFC HQ there be raised to the status of a Division, with a Major General in command. Allenby then added the special request of Geoffrey Salmond to return to Egypt to take command of the Royal Flying Corps Middle East. The War Office, still drunk from Allenby's remarkable victory were more than happy to honor Allenby's request. Major General Geoffrey Salmond departed for Egypt on Christmas Eve.[6] Upon his return, Salmond got to work preparing for Allenby's next offensive--the march towards Damascus. To do this, the RFC Middle East would have to control the skies and keep the enemy's aircraft out of action before and during the advance.

Equipment

British

In this phase of the operations in Egypt and Palestine, the RFC received the tools they so desperately needed. Single seat fighters such as Sopwith Camels and S.E. 5s (See Appendix B) provided the RFC with aeroplanes that were at least a match, if not superior to the machines in the German Air Service. These new British fighters were faster and nimbler than their German counterparts, and the Middle East Division of the RAF received them in sufficient quantities to be a credible threat. By June 1918, the Middle East Division RAF possessed 49 modern fighters and over 190 reconnaissance aircraft.[7]

In addition to the new fighters, the Middle East Division received a Handley Page Bomber in August 1918. This machine, a large four-engine bomber, was capable of long distance bombing while carrying large payloads (see appendix B). This aircraft gave the EEF real aerial offensive capability. It was used decisively at the opening of the Battle of Megiddo to destroy the key communication centers for the enemy's General Headquarters. By the time the Battle of Megiddo began, the quality and quantity of the aircraft available in the Middle East culminated. All the latest and greatest tools of the time were available to Middle East Division RAF, and they made good use of them.

German

The German Air Service continued to field the most modern equipment in their arsenal throughout this phase of operations in Palestine. They were equipped with Rumpler C.4s, Halberstadts, Fokker E-IIIs, and Albatross fighters (see appendix B). However, they did not receive them in quantities that were comparable to the numbers that the British were fielding in this theater, nor did the Germans possess a logistic system for repair parts and maintenance that was comparable to the British. They had to rely upon the supplies sent by way of the Anatolian railway from Constantinople, much of these supplies were diverted to the Caucuses.[8] The fact remains that the Germans did not lose their edge in the quality of aircraft that they supplied to the Palestine theater. Instead, the German Air Service suffered an erosion of air parity in Palestine due to the quantity of aircraft they could maintain in the air, as well as the deterioration of the health and nerve of the German pilots.

Training and Tactics

The Gosport School

The most significant development in this phase of the war was the improvement of flight training for military pilots. In 1916, Major R. R. Smith-Barry was given command of No.1 Reserve Squadron at Gosport. Smith-Barry had received his flight certificate in 1911, and served with Nos. 5 and 60 Squadrons in France before returning to Britain in December 1916. He was taking with him two years of experience in the development of aerial combat techniques and procedures.[9]

By late 1916, there was still a lot about aeroplanes and flying that were mysteries. Although there was a consensus among pilots and trainers at the time regarding certain control inputs and their anticipated results, there were some activities related to flight that were regarded as anomalies, even as acts of God. One such eventuality was the phenomenon of spinning. Up until 1916, most pilots who had the unfortunate fate of entering a spin never regained control and met their deaths. There were a few notable exceptions. While in France, Major J. A. Chamier emerged from a cloud in a spin. While falling helplessly, Chamier recalled an incident that occurred before the war, when

Lieutenant W. Parke recovered his aeroplane from a spin very near the ground. When he emerged from the cockpit, Lieutenant Parke admitted that he managed to recover the aircraft by doing "everything wrong."[10] Chamier did the opposite of what his experience as a pilot would have otherwise suggested and he recovered the aeroplane. He referred his story to the Headquarters of the RFC.

This experience began to reveal that there were no anomalies to flight, all flight characteristics could be explained and controlled. This was proven to Smith-Barry himself when he was introduced to Captain R. Balcombe-Brown, a New Zealand pilot from No. 1 Squadron (while Smith-Barry was still serving with the No. 60 Squadron in France). Balcombe-Brown claimed to have discovered how to initiate a spin as well as emerge from one. Smith-Barry was skeptical, but followed the directions given by the New Zealander, as did several of his pilots. To their astonishment, Balcombe-Brown was right. According to the official record of the war in the air, it was the explanation of maneuvers such as controlled spins, that became the "key-note" of the Smith-Barry system.[11]

When Smith-Barry took over the No. 1 Reserve (Training) Squadron at Gosport, he began to foster his ideas regarding the aeroplane and flight. According to one of his instructors at the time:

> The gospel he preached was that the aeroplane was a nice tempered, reasonable machine that obeys a simple honest code of rules at all times and in any weather. And by shedding a flood of light on the mysteries of its control he drove away the fear and the real danger that existed for those who were flying aeroplanes in the blackest ignorance even of first principles.[12]

As a result of his successful techniques, which were rapidly becoming known throughout the RFC, Major Smith-Barry was given free reign to develop his ideas and create a school for "Special Flying." As a result, the Gosport School was formally established in August 1917. The first task of the school would be to educate the flying instructors, who would in turn impart these methods upon their student pilots. In October 1917 a pamphlet was circulated entitled, *General Methods of Teaching Scout Pilots*. This pamphlet had the effect of initiating the transformation of training principles and techniques long before the instructors were circulated throughout the breadth of the Royal Flying Corps.[13]

Another booklet entitled simply, *Flying Instruction*, detailed the principles developed at the Gosport School and was widely disseminated throughout the newly formed Royal Air Force from the Spring of 1918 and onwards.[14] The Gosport school was quickly gaining attention for its revolutionary training methods. John Salmond, Geoffrey's younger brother (also an RFC pilot), visited the Gosport School and adopted the method for use in all pilot training schools in Britain.[15] At the time, Major General John Salmond was in command of the Training Division in Britain. It was these efforts that standardized and greatly enhanced the instruction that pilots received. As a result, Britain began to produce more competent pilots from the schools who arrived at their operational squadrons with at least better than rudimentary skills in the ways of aerial combat.

The Formation of the Training Group in Egypt

The changes in pilot training that were sweeping through Britain in 1917 were also felt in Egypt. Whether it was due to the communication of ideas that the Gosport School fostered or whether it was due to the personal relationship between Geoffrey Salmond and his younger brother John--who happened to be in charge of the Training

Division in Britain--is uncertain. What is known is that the Training Brigade expanded greatly in 1917.

In July 1917, the British Government decided to double the size of the Royal Flying Corps. As a result, the War Office decided, once again, to take advantage of the favorable flying conditions in Egypt. In August 1917, the Thirty-Second Training Wing was established in Egypt. Therefore by September 1917 there existed three reserve wings in Egypt: the Thirty-eighth at Heliopolis, the Thirty-Second at Ismailia, and the Twentieth at Abu Qir. The Thirty-second and Twentieth wings contained an elementary squadron and three higher training squadrons each. On 1 November 1917, the three training wings along with the Cadet Wing and School of Aeronautics became a Training Group under the command of Colonel P. L. W. Herbert. Colonel Herbert was a commander of a training group in Britain and was freshly conversant in the ideas and techniques that were being implemented there.[16] What this meant for the RFC Palestine Brigade was that there was a "fresh bench" of pilots from which to draw.

Organization and Operations

"Bloody April" 1917.

In the latter part of 1916, the Germans began to put together the elements of what would become known as "*Jastas*" which was short for *Jagdstaffeln* which is translated as "hunting echelons." These were fighter-pure formations developed to wrestle air superiority away from the allies. The tool intended to get this job done was the Albatross D.I. The first *Jasta* made its debut on Sunday, 17 September 1916. It pounced on two British flights of B.E.2c and F.E.2b aircraft and cut them to pieces.[17]

The Royal Flying Corps' offensive strategy was to render the German air service ineffectual by continually flying on the German side of the lines. While this might be a feasible strategy if the RFC possessed equipment that was at least equal to or superior than that of the Germans, by late 1916 the British D.H.2s and two seat reconnaissance aeroplanes were no match for the Albatross series of aeroplanes that were beginning to patrol the skies over the front.

The Germans fielded over thirty *Jastas* on the western front by the Spring of 1917. These squadrons, now equipped with Albatross D.IIIs, "played havoc" on the RFC who continued to cross the German lines as part of their offensive plan. Almost every time they did so, they were cut down. Things were not much better on the front in Palestine, but they were about to improve.

Reorganization of EEF

When General Allenby assumed command on 28 June 1917, he immediately set out to inspect and evaluate the status of his force and weigh it against the task of winning an offensive in Palestine. He sent a cable to London on 12 July with his assessment. He requested two additional divisions, as well as additional artillery, and aircraft. He proposed to form two infantry corps and one cavalry corps all under a general headquarters. In support of this force, he requested three additional aircraft squadrons so that he would have a squadron in support of each corps, one for the general headquarters, and one fighter squadron. He added that the aircraft should be of the latest type.[18] The request was approved and the additional forces began to flow in almost immediately.

72

Capture of Beersheba

Following the failure of the second attack on Gaza by Murray, what ensued was six months of trench warfare. In which each side conducted sporadic bombardments and raids on the other, while continuing to reinforce and improve defensive positions. It was similar to the trench warfare that had evolved on the Western front in Europe, except for an important consideration. While the Turkish line was dug in and tied to the Mediterranean coast at Gaza, its left flank was tied in to Beersheba, and that is where the trench-line ended (see figure 7).

On 5 October 1917 General Robertson sent a telegraph to Allenby explaining that the War Cabinet had "insisted upon the desirability of eliminating Turkey from the war at a blow. It was thought that her general condition was now such that a heavy defeat. . .might induce her to break with her allies."[19] Allenby, while asking for reinforcements and additional equipment, devised his plan for the attack based upon the means at his immediate disposal. His intention was to take Gaza, but not by a direct assault upon it. Instead, Allenby intended to attack the enemy's weak flank at Beersheba first, consolidate on the objective and attack against Gaza from the West and Northwest.[20]

The operation depended upon the swift capture of Beersheba, while it was un-reinforced. Surprise, therefore, would be key. Allenby explained to General Chauvel, Commander of the Desert Mounted Corps, that he needed to be in position both Southwest and East of Beersheba before the enemy had time to realize from where the attack would come. The risk was that any hint at a large attack against Beersheba might cause the enemy to withdraw from Beersheba and reinforce Gaza. Allenby's plan for achieving surprise was through successful counter-reconnaissance and the use of deception.

According to the official history of the EEF, the enemy commander of the Sinai Front informed the Yilderim Group Command on 19 September 1917 that "the mastery of the air has unfortunately for some weeks completely passed over to the British."[21] The RFC was succeeding in keeping the enemy insulated from the movement of the British formations. Furthermore, Allenby was holding a few Bristol fighters in reserve until a few days prior to the attack when he intended to intensify the air campaign against the enemy. According to the official record of the EEF:

In all, ninety-three enemy machines were brought down, fifty-nine of them behind the enemy's lines, eleven in our own lines, and twenty-eight out of control. Our long distance reconnaissance machines, which on previous occasions had been attacked on sight by the enemy, were now carefully avoided by him.[22]

The enemy's reconnaissance efforts would not unveil Allenby's plan. Furthermore, Allenby used deception to keep the enemy's focus away from Beersheba.

On 10 October, an officer from the G.H.Q. staff rode out into No Man's Land with a small escort, and was fired on by a Turkish cavalry patrol. The officer feigned being wounded and dropped his field glasses and a haversack containing bundles of papers that he had previously stained with blood from his horse. The papers that were in the sack were mock agendas for G.H.Q. conferences which indicated that the main attack would be carried out against Gaza, while feints were launched against Beersheba. There were other documents, personal effects, ciphered messages, and money to convince the Turks that the haversack was genuine. According to the official history of the Palestine campaign, Kress von Kressenstein himself believed in the authenticity of the "captured documents". In fact, even after the attack on Beersheba had begun, Kress refused to send reinforcements and simply ordered that "Beersheba [will] be held."[23]

On 21 October, the first movements of the Desert Mounted Corps were initiated. The intent was to give this force ten days to take up positions South of Beersheba at Khelasa and Asluj. The Australian and New Zealand Mounted Division moved mostly at night and hid in the Wadis during the day. Although the enemy must have been aware of some movement, the Turks never identified the size of the force that was assembling South of Beersheba.

On one particular occasion, the RFC's successful counter-reconnaissance efforts became evident. On 30 October, a German reconnaissance aircraft managed to use sparse cloud cover to infiltrate across the lines and reconnoiter the now prepared British forward attack positions. As the reconnaissance pilots attempted to re-cross the lines back to their base, they were found and pounced upon by a patrolling Bristol fighter and shot down. The Germans tried to escape once on the ground but were captured. Found in their possession were photographic plates, marked maps and notes--information that might have had a devastating affect on Allenby's plan.[24] In all, there were seven encounters with enemy aeroplanes from 28 to 31 October, but the German pilots retreated on all occasions.[25]

The attack began at 5:55 am on the morning of 31 October 1917 with an artillery bombardment of the Turkish positions at Beersheba. The XX Corps initiated their movement by 07:00 and before the day was out, Beersheba was in British hands--the final assault being a cavalry charge of the 4th Lighthorse Brigade. The XX Corps captured 2,000 prisoners and thirteen guns.

Capture of Gaza

While Beersheba was secured by the British, the high ground North of Beersheba as well as Gaza remained to be captured. The defenses of Gaza were a series of positions and trenches stretching from the Mediterranean Sea along the Gaza-Beersheba road for approximately thirty miles. By now, Gaza was a fortress, defended by three Turkish divisions. Opposing them were the British XXI Corps supported by nine Naval gunboats off the coast of Gaza and two RFC squadrons.

The attack on Gaza began on the evening of 1 November 1917 at 23:00. It was initiated with an artillery bombardment from land and sea on the Gaza defensive positions. Approximately 10,000 British infantry took part in the assault against approximately 4,500 Turkish defenders, who were reinforced by approximately 3,500 additional infantry (approximately 8,000 Turkish rifles in all). The assault on Gaza was a coordinated advance from the South of the city as well as from the newly held positions at Beersheba to the West. The British defeated a Turkish attempt at a counter-attack on 5 November, and by 7 November the fall of Gaza was secured by an early morning bayonet charge.[26]

The Turkish retreat made all the more difficult with the RFC continuously attacking their retreating columns throughout 7 and 8 November.[27] While using the RFC for attacking retreating formations was the subject of much debate at the air headquarters, a unique capability had been created for the Commanding General of the RFC-Middle East. The existence of the training units in Egypt gave the air commander the ability to drawn upon those units to form an independent bombing reserve at his disposal when he deemed it necessary. No. 23 Training Squadron, consisting of B.E.2e and B.E.12 aircraft, was formed to do just that and arrived from Egypt on 30 October. It was stationed at Weli Sheikh Nuran, approximately twenty miles Southeast of Gaza and remained there until early December 1917.[28] This unit played an important role in the air offensive that ensued following the seizure of Gaza, conducting ground-attack and bombing operations against enemy positions and retreating formations.

A remarkable bombing attack was carried out on 9 November. As part of their withdrawal, German airmen concentrated with their equipment and associated personnel at an aerodrome at Et Tine. This aerodrome was the target of a large bombing mission consisting of twenty-two bombers with an escort of fighters. The mission dropped a total of 128 bombs on the enemy positions. This attack had a tremendous effect on the enemy's morale as evidenced by von Kressenstein's remarks, "On the afternoon of the 9th of November there broke out a panic at Et Tine. . . . This did more to break the heart of the Eight Army and to diminish its fighting strength than all the hard fighting that had gone before."[29] The RFC-Middle East, as well as Allenby took very keen note on the effectiveness of aircraft on the retreating enemy. When troops on the ground were in position to take advantage of such a panicked flight--the annihilation of an army is entirely possible.

Capture of Jerusalem

As the Turks fled, Allenby's forces pursued. The Turks offered some sporadic resistance as they retrograded. At Junction Station the Turks managed to offer a coordinated and organized defense. The 75th Division halted West of Junction Station for the night. Early the next morning, 14 November 1917, the Turks abandoned their defense at Junction Station and the 75th Division moved in and occupied the station. The Turks were now broken into two groups, one fleeing north and the other east. The reports at the time indicated that the groups were small and scattered and not likely to offer an organized defense.[30] Overall the EEF had advanced sixty miles in fifteen days and drove an enemy of nine infantry and one cavalry division out of entrenched positions they had defended and improved for six months. The EEF gave battle during the pursuit wherever the opportunity arose. The enemy lost almost two-thirds of its force following the capture of Gaza and the pursuit. In all, over 9,000 Turkish prisoners, 80 artillery pieces, 100 machine guns, and large quantities of ammunition and supplies were captured.[31]

Allenby's forces continued the pressure on the fleeing Turks fighting and defeating the forces they met in Jaffa, Judea, Auja, and on the outskirts of Jerusalem. By

1 December, the EEF was solidifying its positions around Jerusalem and converging on the holy city. The date of the attack was set for 8 December 1917. On 7 December, the favorable weather that the EEF had been graced with during their rapid movement through the desert finally broke. It rained almost continuously for three days. This made the flow of supplies to the attacking forces very difficult as the roads became almost impassable.[32] It also meant that the RFC could not get planes in the air to assist with the attack or to provide intelligence regarding the Turkish positions and movements. No. 113 Squadron sent up one aeroplane for a reconnaissance on 8 December, flown by their Squadron commander himself.[33]

The attack began at dawn on 8 December 1917--in spite of the heavy rains. By evening the Turks lost their hold on Jerusalem and fled to the hills north and east of the city. As they fled, No. 14 Squadron manhandled their aeroplanes to the top of a small steep hill in order to give the pilots a flying start. In this manner the squadron managed to fly fifty hours, dropping approximately 100 twenty-pound bombs on the fleeing and demoralized Turks.[34] These ground attacks on the Turks continued from 10 through 12 December. The EEF occupied a line across the Nablus-Jerusalem road four miles north of Jerusalem, as well as a position east of Jerusalem across the road to Jericho. Jerusalem was isolated by the morning of 9 December, the city surrendered at about noon.[35]

On 11 December 1917, General Allenby walked through the Jaffa gate into the holy city of Jerusalem. According to the official history, "He was conducted to the steps of the citadel, where the notables of the city awaited him. A proclamation was read, and after the chief inhabitants had been presented, the commander-in-chief passed out again the way he had come."[36] The Turks suffered heavy casualties in the conduct of this operation, but nothing could compare to the impact that this British victory had on the morale of the Turkish soldiers and leaders. The strategic blow to Turkey was significant, but they were not yet finished. At Jerusalem, the EEF consolidated their forces and prepared for the next advance against the Turks.

Summary

The success that Allenby was able to achieve at Beersheba, Gaza and Jerusalem depended heavily on the fact that the enemy was thoroughly deceived and overwhelmed. The RFC succeeded in denying the enemy the ability to conduct aerial reconnaissance and therefore kept them blind to the movements and intentions of Allenby's forces. This is the key. It is not enough to have superiority in the air, what the RFC achieved in this phase was dominance of the aerial reconnaissance role.

After Jerusalem, the RFC did not sit on its laurels. Instead, the newly formed RFC Middle Eastern Division continued to put pressure on the German Air Service in Palestine. By the time Allenby was ready to launch his final offensive in Autumn 1918, the German Air Service was effectively shut down. In nine months, the RFC achieved mastery of the skies over Palestine.

---

[1]Bourne, *Who's Who in World War One*, 5-6.

[2]T. E. Lawrence, *Seven Pillars of Wisdom* (New York: Random House, 1926), 383.

[3]Baker, A., 110.

[4]Ibid., 116.

[5]Ibid., 115.

[6]Ibid., 120.

[7] H. A. Jones, *The War in the Air,* vol. 6: Appendices (Oxford: Clarendon Press, 1937), Appendix XL.

[8] General Liman Von Sanders, *Five Years in Turkey* (Annapolis: The United States Naval Institute, 1927), 255.

[9] Jones, *The War in the Air*, vol 5., 429.

[10] Ibid., 430.

[11] Ibid., 431.

[12] Ibid.

[13] Ibid., 432.

[14] Ibid., 445.

[15] Baker, A., 88.

[16] Jones, *The War in the Air*, vol. 5, 453.

[17] Thomas R. Funderburk, *The Early Birds of War: The Daring Pilots and Fighter Aeroplanes of World War I* (New York: Grosset & Dunlap, 1968), 93.

[18] Jones, *The War in the Air*, vol. 5, 225.

[19] Falls, 27.

[20] Brian Gardner, *Allenby of Arabia* (New York: Coward-McCann, Inc, 1965), 125.

[21] H. Pirie-Gordon, ed., *A Brief Record of the Advance of the Egyptian Expeditionary Force, June 1917 to October 1918*, 2nd ed. (London: H.M. Stationary Office, 1919), 112.

[22] Ibid., 112.

[23] Falls, 43.

[24] Jones, *The War in the Air*, vol. 5, 236.

[25] Ibid., 239.

[26] Pirie-Gordon, 5.

[27] Ibid., 6.

[28]Jones, *The War in the Air*, vol. 5, 241.

[29]Ibid., 243.

[30]Ibid., 247.

[31]Pirie-Gordon, 7.

[32]Ibid., 9.

[33]Jones, *The War in the Air*, vol. 5, 248.

[34]Ibid., 248.

[35]Pirie-Gordon, 10.

[36]Jones, *The War in the Air*, vol. 5, 249.

CHAPTER 5

THE BATTLE OF MEGIDDO

Airpower Before the Battle

By the dawn of the new year, 1918, Allenby had achieved everything he had been

asked to do. Robertson and the War Cabinet, as well as the Prime Minister Lloyd George

himself had wanted "Jerusalem by Christmas," and now they had it. Furthermore,

Allenby had established a line from Jaffa to Jerusalem. Now the EEF needed to

consolidate its resources and make preparations for the next attack which was intended to

drive the Turks all the way to Damascus. However, the Prime Minister wished for

Allenby to attack immediately with the belief that Turkey could be pushed out of the war

in a matter of weeks.[1] Allenby, known to be aggressive and unrelenting in his pursuit of

the enemy, was also prudent and never promised more then he thought he could deliver.

He knew the importance of preparation, especially in the sparse and unforgiving desert

climate. In January he explained to Robertson that with the forces he had at his disposal

he could clear Palestine by the summer. If an advance further than that was required--to

Aleppo or beyond--an additional sixteen divisions would be needed.[2] This request, of

course, was outrageous considering the Allied position in early 1918.

Despite the success that Allenby and Britain enjoyed at the close of 1917, the fact

that the Russian Revolution had removed Russia from the war was to have a dramatic

impact on the spring of 1918. German troops streamed from the Eastern Front to join in

on the Ludendorff offensives of spring 1918. Ludendorff was determined to have an

impact before the influence and pressure of the American troops could be felt. Likewise,

Britain was redistributing its forces in order to meet the Germans massing along the

Western Front. Allenby would have to send forces back to Europe in order to support the defensive efforts there. Therefore, instead of receiving additional forces for the offensive operations he was planning, he was losing forces. Allenby sent two full divisions (the 52nd and 74th), twenty-four British battalions from his other divisions, as well as nine Yeomanry regiments, five heavy artillery batteries and five machine-gun companies. In all 60,000 troops were sent from Egypt to Europe.[3]

General Jan Christian Smuts was dispatched from the War Office to examine the situation in the Middle East and to send back his assessment. Allenby received Smuts cordially and within a month Smuts cabled home his assessment which agreed with everything that Allenby had said.[4] Furthermore, since the Western Front was having a considerable drain on manpower and resources from the Middle East, it was quite impossible to continue offensives in both Palestine and Mesopotamia. Smuts recommended that the offensives in Mesopotamia be sacrificed and that the troops and resources from that front be sent to reinforce the EEF in Palestine.[5]

Allenby and his staff continued to plan for the autumn 1918 offensive. Furthermore, he received reinforcements and replacements in the form of three infantry divisions and a cavalry brigade from Mesopotamia, as well as an Indian cavalry division from France.[6] There were still well over 250,000 British troops in Egypt and Palestine which formed the nucleus of Allenby's divisions. These troops were reinforced by Indian and other forces (such as troops from Australia, New Zealand, Hong Kong, Singapore, France, Italy and South Africa). There were even three battalions of Jewish soldiers sent to Allenby as a result of the Balfour Declaration.[7] Serving with one of these battalions was a young David Ben Gurion, who would eventually become the Prime Minister of Israel.

The re-organization of the EEF continued throughout much of the summer. By the autumn of 1918, Allenby's force consisted of the Desert Mounted Corps (under Lieutenant-General Sir Harry Chauvel), the XX Corps (under Lieutenant-General Sir Philip Chetwode), and the XXI Corps (under Lieutenant-General Sir E.S. Bulfin). By the eve of the offensive the EEF had a total force of about 12,000 cavalry, 57,000 infantry, 540 guns and 350 machine guns.[8] But there were changes also taking place in the camps of his enemy.

On 1 March 1918, General Liman von Sanders replaced General von Falkenhayn. Like Allenby, von Sanders was an old cavalryman, with a keen knowledge of the Turks and a knack for fighting defensive operations. In fact, he was considered to be one of the best defensive generals of his day. He quickly assessed the situation he faced along the Palestinian front:

> Hence there were two battle districts: the land west of the Jordan, where by far the greater part of the British Army in Palestine confronted us, and the land east of the Jordan, where the Arabs were making war against us, led by the British and assisted with every kind of war material.[9]

Von Sanders had two armies under his command, the Seventh and Eighth. He also controlled part of the Fourth Army headquartered in Damascus for purposes of supply. Sanders set to work immediately to reinforce his positions all along the Palestinian front-- calling all effective troops within the control of the Army Group to move to the front lines.[10] By the eve of the offensive the Yilderim had a force of approximately 3,000 cavalry, 23,000 infantry, 340 guns, and 600 machine guns. There were an additional force of approximately 6,000 infantry and some cavalry troops were occupied with the Arab siege of Maan or along the rail line to Dera out in the eastern desert.[11]

In the mean time, Major General Geoffrey Salmond was back in the saddle, commanding the newly expanded Middle East Division of the Royal Air Force. He now had sufficient numbers of the most state-of-the-art aircraft available from Britain: Bristol fighters, RE8s, and Vickers Bullets. Salmond was determined to dominate the skies over Palestine and Egypt and keep the German air service from flying during the autumn offensive. This was a lofty goal and one that had to be acted upon immediately if it was to be achieved. August would prove to be the decisive month for the RAF British pilots were continuously in the air and gave chase to any enemy machine they encountered regardless of the type or number. According to captured enemy documents the British pilots were having an extraordinary effect on the German Air Forces: 25 August 1918-- "In consequence of lively hostile flying activity, no reconnaissance could be carried out."[12]

Salmond was achieving the effect he desired. Later in the year, he described in a lecture that, "In August 1918 the Palestine Brigade had attained mastery of the air. By this I mean that although occasionally German machines did fly, if they once saw our machines they never fought, but went to ground, the personnel ran off."[13] By the end of August 1918, over ninety German aircraft had been destroyed. By suffering losses they were unable to quickly replace and by the effect that the Royal Air Force was having on the enemy's morale--the German Air Service in Palestine was effectively being shut down.

The timing of this effect was critical. Allenby was planning for his operation to commence on 19 September 1918, but was still considering the exact execution of the attack. His first plan, briefed in strict secrecy to his three corps commanders on 1 August 1918, conceived of the XXI Corps attacking on the enemy's right flank with five infantry divisions, the Desert Mounted Corps would then advance through the gap provided by the XXI Corps and proceed up the Plain of Sharon to the Nahr Iskanderune line (a streambed running from Tul Karm to the Mediterranean Sea). The mission of the DMC would be to protect the XXI Corps left flank and to advance onto Sebustiye (Samaria) thereby sitting astride the Nabulus-Tul Karm railway and road networks; meanwhile the XX Corps would attack astride the Nabulus road.[14] This scheme was bold and, if successful, would trap a considerable portion of the Turkish forces and cut an important logistic line.

After three weeks of contemplation, however, Allenby altered his plan and on 22 August 1918 briefed his commanders that he decided to expand the scope of the operation.[15] The first step would occur on the night preceding the main attack--in which the XX Corps would advance up to positions east of the Bireh-Nabulus road in order to defend the right flank of the main attack and to prevent the enemy exits into the lower Jordan valley. The main attack would still be initiated by the XXI Corps under Bulfin, whose task would be to break through the enemy defensive line from the railway at Tul Karm to the sea. Once through, the XXI Corps would turn right and continue to advance in a northeasterly direction towards Samaria and Attara. Meanwhile, the Desert Mounted Corps, with their gap now open between Tul Karm and the Mediterranean Sea, was to advance across the Nahr Falik and turn to the right in the vicinity of Jelameh to advance in a northeasterly direction across the hills of Samaria and enter the Plain of Esdraelon at

El Lajjun (Megiddo), the DMC was to then continue along the Plain to seize El Afule and

Nazareth (Yilderim Headquarters) (see figure 8).[16]

In all, this advance of the DMC would be approximately 50 miles. This plan was bold and audacious but relied heavily upon surprise and speed. In order to achieve this, Allenby had to ensure the strictest of secrecy and that his moves remain undetected by the enemy. Allenby had two things going for him in the preparations for his offensive-- Lawrence with the Arab Northern Army, and the Royal Air Force.

The Arab Northern Army was carrying out incursions and ambush attacks against the Turks in the vicinity of Amman and as far north as Dera. These attacks proved to be frustrating to the German staff and damaging to their logistics and communications. But more importantly the actions of the Northern Arab Army served to tie up considerable numbers of Turkish troops and provided a great concern to von Sanders himself who expressed his concern in a letter to Ludendorff, in which he stated that he "had to expect a big attack in the coast sector" but believed that his forces could "weather it."[17] His greatest concern, therefore, was to the east where his lines of communication to Damascus were in jeopardy and where he believed that the British might exploit his relative weakness. He stated "the constantly increasing force of the hostile Arabs held the shortest line to these communications."[18] The Northern Arab Army was providing Allenby with his operational diversion.

The Royal Air Force, as previously mentioned, had attained "mastery of the air" by the end of August 1918. This is evidenced by the significant reduction in German reconnaissance missions over the lines. In June 1918, Yilderim aircraft crossed over the EEF's lines approximately 100 times. By the last week in August 1918, the number of crossings was reduced to 18. And during the first three weeks in September, only 4 enemy aircraft flew across the EEF lines.[19] The Royal Air Force-Middle East Division forward deployed the Palestine Brigade which consisted of two wings supporting the offensive--the Fifth and Fortieth Wings. Squadrons occupied and operated from aerodromes in Sarona, Ramle and Jerusalem. From these locations, the RAF remained within 10 miles of the front lines, while the German aerodromes at Jenin and Elfule were 25 to 40 miles away respectively.

To support the offensive, the Palestine Brigade was organized as follows. The Fifth Wing was headquartered in Ramle with its three squadrons divided out, each in support of a corps: No. 14 Squadron supporting XX Corps from Junction Station; No. 113 Squadron supporting the XXI Corps from Sarona; and No. 142 Squadron supporting the Desert Mounted Corps also from Sarona. The No. 142 Squadron also sent one flight out to support Chaytor's Force which was anchored into the Dead Sea and defending a line along the West Bank of the Jordan River. This flight in support of Chaytor operated from Jerusalem. Furthermore, No. 142 Squadron would move up to, occupy and operate from the Turkish Aerodrome at Jenin once it was captured. The task and purpose of these corps squadrons would be to conduct artillery cooperation, contact patrols and tactical reconnaissance out to a distance of ten thousand yards in front of the advancing forces.[20]

The Fortieth Wing was also headquartered at Ramle, its responsibility would be to support the EEF headquarters. It consisted of three squadrons which would conduct strategic missions. The No. 1 Squadron (Australian Flying Corps) was responsible to conduct strategic photography and reconnaissance from Ramle; the No. 111 Squadron (the newly formed fighter squadron) was to provide escort for reconnaissance missions as well as offensive patrols from Ramle; and the No. 144 Squadron was to conduct strategic bombing operations from Junction Station. Furthermore, it was stressed to the ground forces that the Turkish aerodromes and landing grounds were to remain clear of traffic and bivouacs so that they may be put into use as quickly as possible.[21]

As Allenby concentrated his forces and put all the pieces in place to launch his offensive, concealment of his movements became his most critical concern. No movement was to be conducted at concealed bivouacs between 0430 and 1830. And if it was absolutely necessary to water the horses during the day it would be done between 1200 and 1400, at which time the RAF would increase patrols to fend off enemy reconnaissance efforts. No fires were to be lit, and the RAF would fly over and photograph each artillery and gun emplacement in order to determine if the locations were sufficiently camouflaged or otherwise recognizable from the air. According to the official history of the battle, "The concealment of the British movements depended, however, rather than upon any other single precautionary measure, on the activity of the Royal Air Force."[22] For these measures as well as for dominating the counter-reconnaissance efforts of the EEF, the RAF Palestine Brigade was indispensable.

In a captured enemy Intelligence Disposition Map issued to the Yilderim Army Group on the day before the offensive, the Yilderim Army Headquarters had the EEF's force distribution completely wrong. It was evident that the Yilderim had no idea of the British moves. The map shows no alteration of forces along the front, nor any concentration of cavalry on the coast. This, in conjunction with the enemy air service reports that "no essential changes had taken place in the distribution of the British Forces,"[23] is evidence to the absolute efficiency and effectiveness of the EEF's concentration of forces and clandestine moves, as well as the complete impotence of the enemy's aerial reconnaissance efforts--the stage was set.

91

Airpower During the Battle

Early on the morning of 19 September 1918, a Handley Page O/400 bomber took off with over one thousand pounds of bombs which it delivered upon the telegraph and telephonic exchange at El Afule. Within five hours five DH9s of No. 144 Squadron attacked the target again, while eight other aircraft attacked von Sanders GHQ at Nazareth. In conjunction with these attacks, No. 142 Squadron bombed the Yilderim 8th Army HQ at Tul Karm and the No. 144 Squadron attacked the 7th Army HQ at Nabulus.[24] The effect of these initial bombing missions was that the Yilderim HQ had virtually no communications with its subordinate Army HQs for the next crucial two days and the enemy would have no knowledge of Allenby's movements.

Major-General Salmond was determined to keep the German air service from playing any role in the offensive. The best way to accomplish this, was to keep them from getting into the air. He kept patrols of two DH9 bombers flying over the airfield at Jenin all day long. Every two hours the two-aircraft contingent was replaced with fresh aircraft and crews. As they departed their patrols, the aircraft dove down and machine-gunned the hangars at Jenin. Furthermore, the patrolling aircraft would drop their bombs on the airfield at he slightest sign of activity. As a result, no German aircraft left that airfield.[25]

The ground campaign began early in the morning of 19 September, at 0430 with a fifteen minute artillery barrage. The preparatory bombardment comprised of an average of one gun per 50 yards and was assisted by the Royal Navy destroyers offshore: *Druid* and *Forester*. In all, an average of one thousand shells per minute were fired, making this the heaviest preparatory bombardment conducted in this theater.[26] The Infantry of the XXI Corps advanced as the creeping barrage opened the way before them. As they attacked forward, three aircraft continually patrolled the area in front of the XXI Corps and conducted artillery cooperative fires against thirty-two active enemy batteries.[27] Due to the reconnaissance efforts of the RAF prior to the offensive, virtually all of the 8th Army's artillery positions were known. As a result, any Turkish artillery that fired against the advancing troops was quickly silenced by devastatingly accurate counter-battery fire. The Turkish positions were quickly overrun and by late afternoon the Turkish XXII Corps and 8th Army headquarters at Tul Karm fell to the EEF XXI Corps. Ultimately, the British captured 7,000 prisoners and 100 guns. The Yilderim XXII Corps ceased to exist.[28]

Remnants of the Turkish Eight Army retreated down the road from Tul Karm to Nablus, in an effort to cross the Jordan. Once the news of the retreat was wired to General Borton, Commander of the Palestine Brigade, the RAF sprung their first planned ground attack operation. Aeroplanes began to bomb and strafe the fleeing Turks from mid-day until dark. Dropping eleven-and-a-quarter tons of bombs and spraying 66,000 machine gun rounds into the Turkish formations.[29] These bombing attacks that began on 19 September became a prominent feature of the offensive and denied the Turks the ability to make an orderly withdrawal.

At 0700 the lead elements of the Desert Mounted Corps, the 5th Cavalry Division, began its march through the gap that the XXI Corps was providing. The 5th Cavalry moved quickly through the breech and overran the light resistance they faced as well as the third line of Turkish defenders. By noon they had traversed 25 miles and took up position southwest of Acre. The 4th Cavalry launched at 0840 and traveled up the length of the Plain of Sharon arriving at the entrance to the Musmuss pass by 1630. After a four-hour halt for water, the 4th Cavalry commander dispatched his lead element into the

Musmuss pass--the 2nd Lancers of the 10th Brigade. The rest of the 4th Cavalry Division

followed in quick succession. By 0330, the 2nd Lancers had emerged from the pass onto

the Plain of Esdraelon, 5 miles from El Afule and 10 miles from the Yilderim General

Headquarters at Nazareth. As they fed and watered their horses, the 2nd Lancers spotted

the Turkish 13th Depot Regiment moving toward the Tel Megiddo. The 13th Regiment

was ordered by von Sanders to block the Musmuss pass. The Lancers sprung into action

by fixing and flanking the Turks. The Turks were surprised and were unable to

concentrate accurate fire against the lancers. After forty-six Turks were trampled and

ridden down with the lance, the remaining 470 Turks surrendered.[30]

In the meantime, elements of the 5th Cavalry Division seized El Afule and

Nazareth by 0715 on the morning of the 20 September. Unfortunately for the EEF, Liman

von Sanders was not found in or around the G.H.Q. The 5th Cavalry soon found itself in

an urban fight in Nazareth, which it would continue to fight for the next two days. By

0800 on the morning of the 20 September, the lead elements of the 4th Cavalry Division

found the 5th Cavalry already at El Afule rounding up the remnants of the Turkish

defenders. The airfield at El Afule was so quickly and effectively captured that two

German aeroplanes were still on the ground and intact when the D.M.C. troops seized it.

In fact, as the D.M.C. troops were securing the airfield a German D.F.W. aeroplane

arrived to deliver two bags of mail for the German headquarters. When the pilot realized

the situation, he tried to take off but was engaged by a gunner from an armored car.

Wounded, both the pilot and observer surrendered.[31] As soon as it was captured and

secured, the RAF began to fly petrol, oil and spare parts into El Afule and turned the

German Aerodrome into a forward staging base for strategic reconnaissance flights.[32] By mid-afternoon, the 4th Cavalry proceeded on to the southeast to close off Beisan and complete the trap. In all, the 4th Cavalry Division, traveled the farthest in the two days of the Desert Mounted Corps' great cavalry charge--riding over 70 miles in 34 hours. For the rest of the day, the 4th and 5th Cavalry Divisions spread out across the rear of the Turkish lines.

The RAF also provided valuable support for the quick moving cavalry. Flying in advance of the D.M.C., No. 113 Squadron flew patrols to provide reconnaissance for the advancing cavalry. In one instance, on the morning of 19 September, a reconnaissance aeroplane from No. 113 Squadron dropped a message to the lead elements of the 5th Cavalry Division. The pilot informed them that there were approximately two hundred infantry laying in wait in an orchard east of Basse el Hindi. The lead Squadron, without waiting for covering fire, attacked at once. After a brief but fierce fight, the squadron captured the orchard, taking about sixty prisoners, two guns and twelve wagons. The audacious squadron suffered two wounded and one killed in the action.[33]

Airpower in Pursuit

Very little was left to chance in the planning for this offensive, to include the pursuit of the enemy in the event of a retreat. It was a model of good staff work. Due to the difficulties of the terrain, the EEF staff identified that escape for the Turkish forces were limited to five routes: (1) Tul Karm to Samaria, (2) Samaria to Jenin, (3) Anebta to Jenin, (4) Nablus through the Wadi Fara to Jisr ed Damiye on the Jordan, and (5) Balata through the Wadi Fara to Beisan. Prior to the offensive the RAF photographed these passes and analyzed them to identify choke points that could be bombed to cut off the

95

Turks in retreat.[34] No. 1 Squadron was given the task to patrol these passes and report back their observations via long range wireless communication.

As the Turkish forces began to flee, the RAF diverted its attention to harass, slow or, in some cases, cut off the enemy's retreat. According to the official history of the EEF, on 20 and 21 September, every available machine was used for bombing the retreating enemy.[35] But the most significant of these efforts was the actions against the retreating Turks in the Wadi Al Fara. The overwhelming success of the RAF in blocking the retreat of the Turkish forces in the Wadi Fara was both controversial as well as demonstrative of the effective use of airpower against a canalized and virtually defenseless enemy.

In the early morning hours of 21 September, a pilot and observer from the No. 1 Squadron, Australian Flying Corps, spotted a column of Turkish moving southeast along the Nabulus-Wadi Fara road. The observer sent a report back to the aerodrome using wireless telegraph.[36] It was urgent that this movement be stopped. While the 4th Cavalry had seized Beisan and was blocking the enemy retreat there, there were no EEF forces in position to close the crossings over the Jordan River. The only option available was the employment of the RAF. All available machines were at once mobilized for the attack.[37]

The priority for the attacks was given to the No. 1 Squadron, Australian Flying Corps using Bristol Fighters carrying eight 20-pound bombs each, No. 144 Squadron using DH9's carrying one 112-pound bomb and eight 20-pound bombs, and No. 111 Squadron using S.E.5s carrying four 20-pound bombs. The attack commenced just after 0600 and increased in tempo throughout the day. They were timed in such a manner that two aircraft arrived over the objective every three minutes to bomb and strafe the column, and that an additional six aircraft arrived every half-hour to attack. These attacks lasted until about noon, at which time ground forces arrived in a position to block the retreating Turks.

In all, 88 bombing and strafing passes dropped nine-and-a-quarter tons of bombs and fired 56,000 machine gun rounds against the Turks retreating in the narrow confines of the Wadi Fara. The initial attacks focused on the lead elements of the column, once these elements where destroyed and there was enough wreckage blocking the rout, the subsequent aircraft strafed and bombed along the column. The way was completely blocked with debris consisting of 87 guns, 55 motor lorries, 4 motor cars, and 932 wagons.[38] Tactfully, the official record is silent in regards to the number of lives lost in the wadi.

By 24 September, nearly all the area west of Amman was cleared of Turkish forces. On 25 September, the head of a mixed column was seen traveling from Amman enroute to Mafrak railway station, located between Amman and Dera. The No. 1 Squadron had a new target. Between 0600 and 0800 on the 25 September, ten aeroplanes from the A.F.C. bombed, strafed and thoroughly demoralized this retreating force. The squadron also went on to attack Mafrak station dropping four tons of bombs and firing 20,000 machine gun rounds into the area in three sequential attacks. Many Turks fled on horse or foot and managed to escape the carnage. Approximately six to seven thousand fugitive Turks, mostly from the Fourth Army managed to escape by way of Dera to Damascus.[39]

The remnants of the Turkish II Corps surrendered to Chaytor's Force at Amman on 28 September, while the rest of the Fourth Army fled towards Damascus. On the morning of the 29 September, a reconnaissance flight from No. 1 squadron reported spotting almost the full strength of the Turkish fugitives on the road twenty miles south of Damascus. At noon, five aeroplanes from No. 1 Squadron bombed these columns, causing the Turks to flee in all directions. On the morning of 1 October, the 3rd Lighthorse Brigade entered the city of Damascus. While some pockets of fighting continued on the outskirts of the city, these were in reality the death throes of the Yilderim.

The EEF continued to pursue the retreating Turks fighting small pitched battles along the way from Damascus through Homs all the way to Aleppo. On 26 October, three Turkish envoys were transported to the British Battleship *Agamemnon*, and after four days of negotiation Turkey signed an armistice on 30 October 1918.[40] Turkey was out of the war.

On 19 February 1919, General Allenby addressed the No. 1 Squadron, Australian Flying Corps in a farewell speech:

> Major Addison, officers and men: It gives me considerable pleasure to have this opportunity of addressing you prior to your return to Australia. We have just reached the end of the greatest war known to history. The operations in this theater of the war have been an important factor in bringing about the victorious result. The victory gained in Palestine and Syria has been one of the greatest in the war, and undoubtedly hastened the collapse that followed in other theaters. This squadron played an important part in making this achievement possible. You gained for us absolute supremacy of the air, thereby enabling my cavalry, artillery, and infantry to carry out their work on the ground practically unmolested by hostile aircraft. This undoubtedly was a factor of paramount importance in the success of our arms here. I desire therefore personally to congratulate you on your splendid work. I congratulate you, not only the flying officers, but also your mechanics, for although the officers did the work in the air, it was good work on the part of your mechanics that kept a high percentage of your machines serviceable. I wish you all bon voyage, and trust that the peace now attained will mean for you all future happiness and prosperity. Thank you, and good-bye.[41]

This is probably the best sentiments expressed by Allenby regarding the part of the RAF in the Palestine campaign. Since he did not keep a journal nor any other record of his thoughts or decisions, the only insights we have into his mind are what is available in the official record of the Egyptian Expeditionary Force and from what can be garnered from letters and speeches such as this one.

----

[1]Gardner, 165.

[2]Ibid., 166.

[3]Baker, A., 131.

[4]Gardner, 167.

[5]Ibid., 167.

[6]Ibid.

[7]Ibid., 168.

[8]David L. Bullock, *Allenby's War: The Palestine-Arabian Campaigns, 1916-1918* (London: Blandford Press, 1988), 127.

[9]Sanders, 201.

[10]Ibid., 203.

[11]Bullock, *Allenby's War*, 127.

[12]Pirie-Gordon, 112.

[13]Baker, 132.

[14]Falls, 448.

[15]Ibid., 449.

[16]Pirie-Gordon, 26.

[17]Sanders, 261.

[18]Ibid., 261.

[19]Bullock, *Allenby's War,* 124.

[20]Falls, 460.

[21]Ibid., 461.

[22]Ibid., 462.

[23]Pirie-Gordon, plate 40.

[24]Bullock, *Allenby's War*, 130.

[25]Baker, A., 134-135.

[26]Bullock, *Allenby's War*, 131.

[27]Pirie-Gordon, 113.

[28]Bullock, Allenby's War, 131.

[29]David L. Bullock, "Swift as Eagles: The Victory of the Royal Air Force in Palestine, 1914-1918." (Ph.D. Diss., Kansas State University, 1995), 456.

[30]Bullock, *Allenby's War*, 133.

[31]Cutlack, 158.

[32]Bullock, "Swift as Eagles," 458.

[33]Falls, 523.

[34]Bullock, *Allenby's War*, 135.

[35]Pirie-Gordon, 113.

[36]Cutlack, 159.

[37]Pirie-Gordon, 113.

[38]Ibid., 113.

[39]Cutlack, 167.

[40]Falls, 620-621.

[41]Cutlack, 171.

CHAPTER 6

THE LEGACY OF MEGIDDO

The legacy of the Battle of Megiddo is a lesson in the proper employment of technology in war--not as a "silver bullet" or panacea, but rather as an enhancement to the ground maneuver plan. Once a particular weapon of war is widely available, neither secrecy nor defensive measures will prevent its exploitation. What is important in the use of technology for war is: rapid adoption of the technology into service; experimentation, trial and professional dialogue in its use; training of operators as well as ground forces in the weapon's relevance; mass production and dissemination; and sensible incorporation of the technology into the organizational force structure. Furthermore, in regards to the dissemination of the technology, it is better to mass many elements in a few places than to attempt to position a few elements over a massive area.

The RAF at the battle of Megiddo illustrated the effectiveness of a well integrated technology. It is not to say that the British were alone in their quest. Most air forces at the time were struggling, with varying degrees of success, to develop and improve aeroplanes while simultaneously trying to integrate them into the war effort. The French developed bomber squadrons and the Germans developed fighter squadrons or *Jastas*. While these were innovative, they were not linked with the ground maneuver plan. Instead, these developments took on lives of their own. What did the French strategic bombing initiatives do for the Nivelle Offensive? And how much did "bloody April" assist the Ludendorff Offensives? The answer is: not much. The reason for this is that these advantages were fleeting, unanticipated and uncoordinated. Conversely, the 1918 gradual intensification of the RAF's air campaign in Palestine was timed to coincide with Allenby's autumn offensive. It was not a separate effort, but was indeed part of Allenby's overall plan. Furthermore, the participation of the RAF in all phases of the offensive further illustrates the comprehensive integration of the RAF with the ground maneuver plan.

The synchronization of air and ground efforts at the Battle of Megiddo presaged the success of concepts such as *blitzkrieg*, combined-arms warfare, and air-land battle. It remains uncertain as to whether the Germans used the Battle of Megiddo as a template for the development of their inter-war doctrine. However, they were on the receiving end of Allenby's offensive and the Battle of Megiddo was decisive. If military history teaches us nothing else, it teaches us that the vanquished are often more observant learners than the victors.

There is much to learn from the study of the Battle of Megiddo. In this microcosm of the First World War, we witness the impact of politics on war and vice-versa. We see the importance of leadership in the development and employment of a military force. We observe the importance of learning for a military organization and the communication of this learning through dialogue, literature and training. Finally, we perceive the importance of timing in the planning and conduct of military operations. Specifically, by studying the Battle of Megiddo we behold the essence of achieving battlespace dominance (local air superiority) and the exploitation of this dominance through a carefully coordinated combined arms effort.

The Battle of Megiddo was neither a lucky stroke nor a "flash in the pan" of history. Instead, it was the gradual culmination of three phases of development for the

British Forces in Palestine. These three phases are distinguished by their unique characteristics of leadership, capabilities (based on equipment, training, and tactics), and operational employment.

In the first phase of operations in Egypt, the British organized a force that was determined to defend. This phase, which spanned from August 1914 to February 1916, was demonstrative of the British attitude. By the time they sent forces to defend their interests in Egypt, specifically the Suez Canal, the British had already suffered some disastrous defeats at the hands of the Germans in Europe. Instead of achieving a quick victory, the British were facing the prospect of a protracted war as the Western Front stabilized and the great wound, that was the network of trenches across the face of the European continent, began to fester.

The force that the British sent to Egypt in 1914 was not one of conquest, but was rather an economy-of-force. The British were not yet interested in destroying the Turkish Army that was massing on the Sinai Peninsula. By November 1914, they were more concerned with just being able to defend their interests in the region. But the British sent something to Egypt that gave their small force the important edge they needed--an aeroplane detachment of the Royal Flying Corps. This small compliment of aircraft served to amplify the British defenses by providing vital aerial reconnaissance. Due to the efforts of this handful of aeroplanes and pilots, the British knew when and where the Turks were moving. Thus, the British had the time to maneuver ground forces in order to counter the Turkish threat. By the end of this first phase of operations in Egypt, the British had learned a valuable lesson in the industrial age of warfare--aerial reconnaissance was critical to an effective defense.

As operations in Palestine transitioned into the second phase, from March 1916 to April 1917, the newly named Egyptian Expeditionary Force began to hone its offensive spirit and take the fight to the Turks. This second phase is characterized by the tempered security of the Suez Canal, the successful expansion of the EEF across the Sinai, and the British attacks against the Turkish force at Gaza. Although their two attacks against Gaza were unsuccessful, this last element of this phase again demonstrated to the British the importance of aerial reconnaissance in the conduct of a defense. This time it was the Turks who benefited from the virtually unmolested aerial reconnaissance provided by their allies in the German Air Service.

Also characteristic of this second phase of operations in Palestine was the introduction of the German Air Service into the theater, equipped with aeroplanes that were superior to those of the Royal Flying Corps. Throughout this phase, the RFC wrestled with the German Air Service for control of the skies. The fact that the RFC could not prevent the Germans from conducting aerial reconnaissance of British formations meant that the ground maneuver plan could not achieve surprise or numerical superiority at the point of attack. This was evident at the battles for Gaza.

The third phase of operations in Palestine, from April 1917 to November 1918, was characterized by a sense of British domination which culminated in the battle of Megiddo in September of 1918. This phase witnessed the gradual and deliberate mastery of the skies by the newly formed Royal Air Force Middle Eastern Division. Equipped with sufficient amounts of the most modern aircraft, which were at least equal to those of the Germans, the RAF succeeded in effectively shutting down the German Air Service.

They accomplished this feat twice during this phase: prior to Allenby's offensive against Gaza /Jerusalem and again during the Battle of Megiddo.

Within each phase of operations in Egypt and Palestine the characteristics of leadership, capabilities and operations were distinct. In the first phase the leadership for the British efforts in Egypt was provided by Lieutenant General Maxwell. While competent and knowledgeable of Egypt, Maxwell was unsatisfied with his assignment and longed to be more integral to the strategic decisions of the war. To his credit, Maxwell established and maintained a robust defense of the Suez Canal, and managed to stave off two large-scale attacks against it. In fact, he laid the foundation for all British efforts in Egypt and Palestine to build upon. Maxwell understood the importance of incorporating aerial reconnaissance into the defense of the Suez Canal, and used all aircraft at his disposal, from both the RFC and RNAS, to accomplish this vital mission. For the duration of his command in Egypt, Maxwell and his British force defended the canal on all sides. He used the RFC's aeroplanes, the only aircraft in theater for much of this phase, to provide early warning and information in support of the defensive measures.

In contrast to Maxwell's defensive posture, the second phase of operations in Egypt and Palestine represented a transition. Lieutenant General Murray pushed his defensive lines out more than 11,000 yards from the canal zone. Once these defenses were completed, Murray decided to drive his Egyptian Expeditionary Force across the Sinai. In so doing, he built a network of logistic nodes as well as a water pipeline across the northern Sinai. This system was vital to the British efforts in the region. In regards to the use of aviation in his efforts, Murray stressed the importance of an air photographic survey and had the RFC cooperate with the topographical section of the intelligence division to produce detailed maps of the featureless desert. This survey and the resultant maps gave the British an important edge in navigating across the Sinai and in establishing detailed plans for follow-on operations. While Murray was enthusiastic and skilled as a commander, he lacked the sizeable force necessary to break the Turkish defenses at Gaza and the aircraft that could challenge and defeat the German Air Service.

Murray's failures at Gaza, coupled with a shift in British strategy regarding the Palestine Theater, ushered in the third phase of operations which was characterized by British domination. Beginning with the appointment of General Edmund H. H. Allenby, the British force in Palestine was being set up for success. Furthermore, the British War office was now ready and prepared to give the EEF all that they needed, within reason, to destroy the Turkish forces in the region and push them out of the war. Allenby's leadership was in stark contrast to his two predecessors. He was cunning, offensive minded and cognizant of the full breadth of warfare in the industrial age. Due to his influence and insistence, the RFC/RAF received sufficient quantities of the most modern aircraft in the British inventory. Armed with these aircraft the RFC/RAF managed to dominate the skies over Palestine, a feat which Allenby exploited and capitalized upon to deceive and defeat the Turkish forces at Gaza, Jerusalem and Megiddo.

While the leadership of the EEF changed with each phase, there was a source of continuity of leadership within the RFC/RAF in Palestine. Geoffrey Salmond came to Egypt in August 1915 and remained until November 1918. He was an enthusiastic leader who not only provided guidance to the air forces under him, but was also an integral part of the fostering of understanding and cooperation between the RFC/RAF and the ground

106

forces. Salmond was involved in all facets of aviation operations in Palestine and was constantly expanding the roles of aeroplanes in the war effort while simultaneously striving to increase the accuracy and effectiveness of the roles that aeroplanes performed. Salmond was instrumental to the overwhelming success of the RFC/RAF in Palestine and is a model of an officer with technical and tactical proficiency, as well as keen sense for the strategic employment of tactical resources. While Allenby's leadership drove the EEF to success over the Turks at Gaza, Jerusalem and Megiddo, it was the remarkable and committed leadership of Salmond that paved the way for Allenby.

While each phase is distinct in terms of leadership, they were also unique in regards to the capabilities that were available or developed during each phase's time period. These capabilities are defined as the equipment, tactics and training available at the time. In the first phase, the aeroplanes introduced into Egypt were extremely rudimentary, comprised of mostly Farmans, Nieuports, and B.E.2s (see appendix B); these aircraft were good enough to be used in aerial reconnaissance roles. Not much more was required of them. In this first phase of operations in Egypt, the Turks did not have any aircraft available to them until the spring of 1916. Therefore, for much of this phase, the RFC enjoyed their solitude in the skies above Egypt and the Sinai.

In the beginning of the second phase of operations in Egypt and Palestine, the edge slipped to the German Air Service. By April 1916 German aircraft were flying reconnaissance in support of the Turks throughout Palestine and the Sinai. These aircraft, mostly Rumplers and Fokker Eindeckers (see appendix B), were superior in speed, performance and firepower, than the aircraft flown by the British from Egypt. These same types of German aircraft were causing havoc in the skies over the Western Front as well. To compensate, the British increased the size of the Royal Flying Corps. They took advantage of the favorable flying weather in Egypt and created a training brigade there, responsible for developing skilled pilots for all theaters of the war. This brigade was a great success. Under the direction of Salmond, it built upon the principles taught at the famous Gosport school in Britain. By the end of this phase, the Egypt Training Brigade was producing over 100 pilots each month. While the quality and quantity of pilots were improving, the aircraft that the British were flying were still inferior to those of the Germans.

In the third phase of operations in Palestine, the RAF matured into a decisive force. Not only was it producing large numbers of skilled pilots, but in 1917 the Palestine Brigade of the RAF finally received aircraft that were more than a match for the German Air Service. Aeroplanes such as the Sopwith Camel and S.E. 5a (see appendix B) arrived in Palestine in quantities that were sufficient to reduce both the size of the German Air Service as well as the morale of the German pilots. Once the RFC/RAF regained its edge in 1917, it held it and honed it until the end of the war. The tenacity and skill of the RFC/RAF pilots coupled with the high quality of aeroplanes with which they were equipped allowed them to wrestle the skies from the German Air Service and achieve complete air dominance in Palestine just prior to the Battle of Megiddo.

In terms of the types of operations that were conducted in Egypt and Palestine, each phase witnessed unique operational postures. The first phase was characterized by a defensive posture, in which the British forces were building up their defenses around the Suez Canal. During this first phase, the British repelled two Turkish attacks from the Eastern Desert as well as attacks from the Western Desert, launched by the Senussi and

108

Sultan of Darfur. The second phase was characterized by a transitional posture in which the EEF secured its defense of the Suez Canal and transitioned to the conduct of offensive operations. As a result, the EEF swept across the northern Sinai up to Gaza, and established a critical logistic support structure in its wake. The third phase was characterized by a culmination of British offensive capability which they brought to bear in a synchronized and coordinated effort against the Turko-Germanic force that opposed them in Palestine.

Throughout all three phases of operations, the support provided by the RFC/RAF in Egypt and Palestine was essential. From the aerial reconnaissance missions in early 1915 that galvanized the British defense of the Suez to the domination of the skies over Palestine in 1918 that facilitated Allenby's maneuver, the RFC/RAF in that theater was an integral part of operations and involved in all levels of planning and coordination.

There is very little scholarship dedicated to the actions of the RFC/RAF in Egypt and Palestine. The sheer number of troops and equipment involved in that theater was a fraction of what was employed on the Western Front. Furthermore, the Western Front was in far closer proximity to the British homeland. For these reasons, the campaigns that were carried out in the other theaters of the First World War are often overshadowed in the analysis of the British actions on the Western Front. And as is often the case, the important lessons of war are misunderstood or unappreciated.

In military operations, the seizure of high ground is often critical to success. The high ground offers the vantage from which to observe enemy movements, increase the strength of the defense, and give impetus to an attack. In the First World War the high ground was in the skies above the terrain, temporarily occupied by each side. But high ground cannot be shared, out of military necessity, it must be seized and exploited. The RAF achieved this at the Battle of Megiddo.

In Palestine, the RFC/RAF demonstrated that the domination of battlespace is not something that can be achieved over-night. Instead, it is a systemic and deliberate process. Furthermore, mastery of the skies is only useful if it is linked to operations on the ground. Due to the capabilities of aeroplanes in the First World War, the sky could not be "occupied" for a prolonged duration of time. Therefore, the command of the air was a tenuous position that was best exploited when it was linked to a ground maneuver plan that focused on speed and maneuver. As the ground forces advanced, the enemy airdromes were captured and the enemy's capability to fight for the skies was further deteriorated. The RAF in cooperation with the EEF achieved this at the Battle of Megiddo. The analysis of the RAF's actions leading up to the Battle of Megiddo is important in understanding the process by which the RAF attained air dominance prior to the battle. Once air dominance was attained, the RAF then demonstrated how airpower could be exploited in all facets of military operations during the Battle of Megiddo.

In the application of military strategy, the knowledge of the enemy is critical. The logical converse to this is also critical--to deny the enemy knowledge of yourself. This is achieved through deliberate, energetic and responsive counter-reconnaissance efforts. By September 1918, the RAF virtually shut down the German Air Service that was providing vital aerial reconnaissance to the Turkish forces. Consequently, the Turks did not possess accurate information regarding the disposition and array of the British forces prior to the battle of Megiddo. Just prior to the attack, Allenby was able to reposition his forces in

110

order to mass more cavalry on his left flank without tipping his hand to the Turks. This was due to the RAF's aggressive counter-reconnaissance patrols.

Communication is vital to the command and control of ground forces. This is especially important once contact is made with the enemy. The aerial bombardment of the telephone and telegraph exchange at El Afule just prior to launching the ground offensive on 19 September 1918, effectively severed communications from von Sanders' General Headquarters to his subordinate commanders.[1] By the time the enemy realized what was happening, it was too late and retreat became the only option.

In order to prevent German aircraft from interdicting or disrupting the EEFs offensive, the RAF maintained a constant presence over the Jenin Aerodrome throughout the first day of the attack. These patrols circled the airfield and attacked any sign of activity at the aerodrome.[2] No German aircraft left the ground that day. The RAF dominated the battlespace.

The role of artillery cooperation during the battle of Megiddo was thorough. Before the offensive, reconnaissance patrols provided extensive photographic coverage of the Turkish artillery positions. These were mapped and prioritized before the battle. During the offensive, reconnaissance aircraft flew in support of each Corps to provide artillery spotting, thereby increasing the accuracy and effectiveness of the British artillery. The thorough work of the RAF before and during the battle of Megiddo increased the lethality of the British artillery to quickly neutralize the Turkish artillery from influencing the battle.

As the Turkish forces pounded a retreat, the RAF again acted decisively. Based on reconnaissance photographs, the RAF had identified possible escape routes for the

Turkish forces. Once reconnaissance aircraft spotted large columns of Turks moving along the Wadi Al Fara on 21 September 1918, the RAF sprang into action. All available aircraft were mobilized to attack the fleeing Turks. The RAF maintained an unrelenting four-hour ground attack on the Turkish column.[3] The Turks were demoralized, dispersed and devastated. The RAF effectively transformed the Turkish retreat into a rout.

In all aspects of the Battle of Megiddo, the RAF demonstrated the enormous capabilities of aircraft when effectively incorporated into the ground maneuver plan. Due to its actions before, during and after the battle, the RAF's dominance of its battlespace was the decisive element that enabled the quick and overwhelming victory of the British over the Turks. While the Battle of Megiddo is a fantastic illustration of combined arms warfare, it was actions of the RAF before, during and after the battle that made it a decisive victory for the British.

Throughout its efforts in Egypt and Palestine, the RFC/RAF evolved as a learning organization spurred on by the competent and committed leadership of people like W. G. H. Salmond, and Edmund Allenby. For the RAF, therefore, the Battle of Megiddo is not only the culmination of their efforts, but it represents the validation of the organizational learning process. As we close this chapter of history and return our focus to the contemporary environment, the thought that lingers is: are the technologies in use today fully integrated and coordinated to achieve operational and strategic goals? Particular technologies and "specialists" are only relevant if they and their efforts are integrated and directed toward a desired endstate. It is up to military leaders to become competent in the breath of full spectrum operations in order to understand when and where to employ technology for decisive effect. This is the legacy of Megiddo.

[1]Pirie-Gordon, 113.

[2]Ibid.

[3]Ibid.

APPENDIX A

HISTORIC MEGIDDO

Solomon

Megiddo reached its peak under Solomon in the tenth century B.C. Solomon

rebuilt Megiddo as a royal city to administer the northern part of the kingdom. During his

reign the city of Megiddo was surrounded by a sturdy casement wall (two parallel walls

with partitions between them, creating rooms). The casements served as barracks or

stables.[1] The Bible records that Solomon fortified the city of Megiddo:

> This is the account of the forced labor that King Solomon conscripted to build the
> house of the Lord and his own house, the Millo, and the wall of Jerusalem, Hazor,
> Megiddo, Gezer . . . as well as all of Solomon's storage cities, the cities for his
> chariots, the cities for his cavalry, and Whatever Solomon desired to build, in
> Jerusalem, in Lebanon, and in all the land of his dominion.

There is no evidence that Solomon ever fought a battle in the Jezreel valley during his

reign, but the fact that he took such effort in fortifying the city of Megiddo suggests that

he was concerned about the need to defend it. While it remains uncertain who he believed

he needed to defend the city against, there is a theory that he was concerned about the rise

to prominence of the Pharaoh Shoshenq I in Egypt. The fact that Shoshenq I lead a

successful campaign into Syria-Palestine five years after Solomon's death in 930 B.C.

and captured Megiddo, among many other cities, echoes the wisdom of Solomon.[2]

Pharaoh Necho II

This chapter of the history of Megiddo is indeed fraught with controversy and

mystery. There are varying accounts of what occurred in 609 B.C., which include the

Bible, Josephus and the Apocrypha. There are slightly differing pictures of the events in the various translations of the Bible and this is the largest source of controversy over the incident.

Necho II was the King of the Twenty-Sixth Dynasty of Egypt. He reigned from 610-595 B.C. In the Spring of 609 B.C. Necho II was answering the call of his Assyrian Ally to fight against the Babylonians. The battle was to take place at Carchemish, located in Northern Syria. This meant that Necho II and his army would have to transverse across the Sinai and all of Palestine and Syria to get there. Necho asked the King Josiah, of Judah, for permission to march through his lands. Instead of granting permission to King Necho, Josiah and his army marched out to the Jezreel valley and awaited the Egyptian army to emerge from the Musmuss Pass.[3]

As the Egyptians gathered in the Jezreel valley the Judean army was arrayed with Josiah in his chariot riding up and down the front lines encouraging his men. Josiah then gave the order to attack. As the battle ensued, Josiah was struck by an arrow and whisked away by chariot. His death marked the end of a brief hope in the rejuvenation of Judah. Furthermore, it marked the beginning of the end for the kingdoms of Israel and Judah. In less than 20 years from Josiah's death, both Israel and Judah would fall to the hands of the Babylonians under King Nebuchadnezzar. He destroyed the city of Jerusalem in 597 B.C. and laid waste to the Temple.[4] Israel and Judah never recovered from that fateful day on the plains of Megiddo.

Saladin

The twelfth century Muslim leader best known for his total annihilation of a Crusader force in 1187 A.D. at the battle of Hattin, was the Kurdish leader known as Saladin. The name Saladin, or Salah ad-Din is an honorific title which translates as *The*

Righteousness of the Faith. This man, who was born in Tikrit in 1138 A.D., was a warrior and General of great renown.[5] He rose to power during the interval between the second and third crusades, after swearing to take back the Holy Land from the Crusaders. Saladin made several forays into the Jezreel valley before and after the Battle of Hattin. In fact, Saladin at least four times repeated the same tactic of crossing Jordan river, entering the Jezreel Valley and harassing the Crusader outposts there.[6]

The Crusaders had an opportunity to learn from an event that occurred in 1183, at a place called Ayn Jalut (the "Spring of Goliath"), located Southeast of Megiddo. When in mid-September of that year, Saladin and his army moved into the Jezreel valley after capturing the city of Aleppo (in modern day Syria) and several cities in Mesopotamia. The Crusaders assembled their force under the command of Guy de Lusignan--a controversial figure whom many of the crusaders considered to be incompetent. The Crusaders moved from their base in Sepphoris to Al-Fula, a city located 10 miles East of Megiddo. The Crusaders then moved on Saladin's army, which was camped at Ayn Jalut, to which Saladin unexpectedly withdrew his forces about one mile away into the open valley near a place called Ayn Tubaniya. The Crusader force occupied Ayn Jalut themselves and remained within sight of Saladin's forces.[7]

Saladin sent forth daily raids, intent on drawing the Crusaders out from Ayn Jalut, but to no avail. Finally, on October 6th, Saladin withdrew his forces to Mount Tabor, perhaps hoping that the Crusaders would pursue him. However, the Crusaders only marched back to Al-Fula before returning to their base at Sepphoris. Saladin re-crossed the Jordan on 8 October and returned with his army to Damascus.[8]

While this event is far from decisive, it was a strategic victory for the crusaders, who only lamented at the fact that Guy de Lusignan failed to attack and defeat Saladin with the largest Crusader army every assembled. The crusaders accused Guy de Lusignan of cowardice. When, in fact, the actions of the Crusaders demonstrated that whenever Saladin's army entered the Jezreel valley it did so with only enough logistics to sustain them for a short while. If the crusader force could continue to prevent Saladin from decisive actions, he may commit a desperate act to force a decision or at least continue to be vulnerable as his supplies were exhausted.

Mamluke Sultan Qutuz

In the thirteen century the Mongol Horde ventured out from the Steppes of Asia and cut a swath of destruction and devastation in their wake. As they moved across the Middle East and into Syria-Palestine, a clash ensued between the Mongols and another revolutionary force--the Mamlukes. The Mamlukes were almost all of Turkish origin who were purchased as children slaves and brought to Egypt. Once there they were converted to Islam and raised under a Mamluke sergeant. Upon reaching adulthood, they were offered their freedom in return for service in the Egyptian army. The Mamlukes were regarded as fierce warriors and were favored by the thirteenth century Egyptian sultans.[9]

Saif ad-Din Qutuz was appointed as regent to the Sultan Aybak in 1253. When the sultan was assassinated in 1257, Qutuz remained as regent for the Sultan's son, al-mansour Ali. Qutuz overthrew Ali in 1259 and made himself Sultan. As such, he raised an army and appointed the Mamluke General Baibars to lead it.[10] Qutuz rejected the Mongol Ambassadors who demanded the Egyptians to surrender, and had the ambassadors executed. Qutuz and his army departed Cairo in July 1260, crossed the

Sinai, marched through Gaza and camped outside of the Crusader city of Acre. There they received food and supplies from the Franks who occupied Acre.

Meanwhile, the Mongols under the command of Kitbuqa marched out from Damascus to meet the advancing Mamluke army. The Mongols took up a position at the city of Ayn Jalut, the same place where the Crusader forces met Saladin in the previous century. Qutuz sent his Mamluke advance guard out under the command of General Baibars, while he led the rest of the army from Acre towards Ayn Jalut. The battle of Ayn Jalut took place on September 3rd, 1260. The fighting was fierce. The Mongols attacked first against the Mamluke left flank. As it gave way, Qutuz reorganized his forces and counterattacked the Mongols, in which he surrounded and overwhelmed them. In the end, Kitbuqa was killed and his decapitated head was sent to Cairo as evidence of the Mamluke victory.[11]

This was the first time that the Mongols were ever defeated in battle. Their air of invincibility was forever shattered. The very course of Western civilization was determined. This great victory of Qutuz, was one that was short-lived. On October 22nd, General Baibars, angered that Qutuz had not appointed him as governor of Syria, assassinated Qutuz and proclaimed himself Sultan.[12]

---

[1]Israeli Foreign Ministry. "Megiddo - The Solomonic Chariot City." Jewish Virtual Library (Available from: http://www.jewishvirtuallibrary.org/jsource/ Archaeology/Megiddo.html, accessed online 24 March 2007).

[2]Cline, 78.

[3]Ibid., 90.

[4]Ibid., 100.

[5]"Saladin," *Wikipedia.com* (Wikimedia Foundation Inc., 2007, available from: http://en.wikipedia.org/wiki/Saladin, accessed online 14 November 2006).

[6]Cline, 126.

[7]Ibid., 133.

[8]Ibid., 134.

[9]Ibid., 144.

[10]"Saladin," *Wikipedia.com.*

[11]Cline, 149.

[12]Ibid., 151.

www.ingramcontent.com/pod-product-compliance
Lightning Source LLC
Chambersburg PA
CBHW081326310526
45789CB00018B/2423